HAIGH

The Mind of a Murderer

Of all the murderers whose exploits have sent shivers down countless spines, Haigh was the most strange. He was the apotheosis of charm, genial, elegantly turned out, with a mildness of manner that accorded well with his religious background, and so fastidious that when he worked in a garage he would not dirty his hands. No wonder spectators at his trial asked how such a man could systematically slaughter people and dissolve them in a bath of acid. Was this man who sat, calm and smiling as he listened to the horrendous account of the prosecution, the perpetrator of such loathsome deeds?

'Fascinating reading' — THE SUNDAY EXPRESS

'Those with a strong stomach should read this remarkable in-depth investigation.' — THE EVENING NEWS

'Macabre yet fascinating.' — THE EVENING STANDARD

Arthur La Bern was born in England of French parents. He began his career as a journalist. He has been crime reporter for *The Evening Standard*, *The Daily Mail* and *The Daily Mirror*, and during the Second World War he was a war correspondent in the Far East. The author of many books including *Hallelujah!* and *Goodbye Piccadilly, Farewell Leicester Square*, on which Alfred Hitchcock's film *Frenzy* was based.

HAIGH

The Mind of a Murderer

Arthur La Bern

A STAR BOOK
published by
W. H. ALLEN

A Star Book
Published in 1974
by W. H. Allen & Co. Ltd.
A division of Howard & Wyndham Ltd.
44, Hill Street, London, W1X 8LB
First published in Great Britain by
W. H. Allen Ltd. 1973

Printed in Great Britain by
Richard Clay (The Chaucer Press), Ltd., Bungay, Suffolk

ISBN 0 352 30025 6

To my friend,
Robert Fabian

Contents

Foreword by Professor Keith Simpson

The case of R v Haigh was a classic in so many of its features that another review adding to the *Notable Trials* edited by Lord Dunboyne, and to that of Miss Lefebure, my secretary at the time, must be welcome. No one has yet penetrated far into the mind of this remarkable killer, and this is undoubtedly the main purpose of Mr La Bern in putting his skilled pen to paper—and securing the professional analysis from Dr Noël Browne which he appends.

Haigh was a shrewd liar, without moral restraints, as his previous record showed. He had successfully disposed of the bodies of at least five other victims by whose deaths, under similar circumstances, he had profited very substantially. Why did he fail with Mrs Durand-Deacon, the rich widow from Kensington? Did he succumb to his own inordinate vanity? Was Dr Yellowlees a wise choice as defence psychiatrist? Was this one of Maxwell Fyfe's poor showings? Or did Hartley Shawcross do as fine an execution for the Crown—and in as few deft and destructive strokes—as we shall ever see? Was that great criminal Judge Travers Humphreys utterly impartial?

Whatever the answers, the case exudes atmosphere, and the author's skill, style and eye for colour gives this new account of the case a freshness and vitality that makes it compelling reading.

Keith Simpson.

Author's Preface

In pursuance of this book I have walked in the footsteps of John George Haigh, one of the most notorious murderers of this century, allegedly one of the most charming and, without doubt, utterly remorseless. I walked in his footsteps from his boyhood home near Outwood Colliery, two miles from Wakefield in Yorkshire, to the Cathedral where, white-surpliced, he sang so sweetly in the choir and served at High Altar. I stayed in the room he occupied at the 'arsenic and old lace' hotel in South Kensington where he picked on his final victim, a colonel's widow. I walked in his footsteps almost to the site of the now happily obsolete scaffold at Wandsworth onto which he stepped, pinioned and smiling even as the hood was slipped over his glossy head and the hangman gave him a reassuring pat on the shoulder before pulling the lever. I have consulted the widow of the chaplain who knelt in prayer with Haigh at the end. I have walked in Haigh's devious footsteps in an attempt to arrive at the basic cause, more than the merely momentary motivation, of his crimes. I sought an explanation beyond the all too facile one that he murdered for profit, as he undoubtedly did, but that is only part of the story.

It is not the profit motive which places Haigh among the more infamous of the world's murderers. Men—and women—have murdered for more lucrative ends and attracted less morbid interest. Haigh gets his niche in infamy because of his particularly nauseating method of disposing of the bodies of his victims.

Yet infamy in itself is not sufficient reason for the literary exhumation of a murderer. Murder in itself is not fascinating, neither is the person who commits it, although there are often circumstances surrounding the crime which invest the perpetrator with an aura akin to a spotlight, deplorable as it might be.

Most murderers—apart from the political ones who have attempted to exterminate entire races or nations—are in themselves insignificant and even inadequate, despite having captured the morbid imagination of the public at the time of their trial. Sometimes, like Crippen, they are to be pitied.

Nobody can pity Haigh. He was himself incapable of pity either for his victims or himself.

Professor Keith Simpson, the eminent pathologist who has kindly provided the foreword to this book, and the man who exhumed Haigh's last victim, described him to me as 'A tough, shrewd little business man.'

Haigh himself gloried in his trial. There is not much doubt that he enjoyed every minute of it. Almost gleefully he wrote to his parents from the prison cell, 'It isn't everybody who can create more sensation than a film star, you know. Even Gorgeous Gussie* would be hard beaten to compete. She's very attractive, isn't she?'

Again he writes, just before his trial for murder at Lewes Summer Assizes, 'I see they are going to run excursions from the South to Lewes next week to see the greatest sensation of the twentieth century. It's certainly more than they would do for Attlee. Only Princess Margaret or Mr Churchill could command such interest.'

Most murderers have one thing in common: a colossal personal vanity. Haigh patently was no exception.

Not only have I walked in his footsteps. I have endeavoured to 'walk' through his mind, believing that it is the duty of laymen

* The glamorous tennis star who created a sensation at Wimbledon by wearing frilly panties.

just as much as medical men and lawyers to fathom what set of circumstances can turn a smiling choirboy into a smiling murderer.

Nearly everybody who knew Haigh was completely baffled. It is too easy to dismiss him as just another 'Jekyll and Hyde'. Even prison officers liked him and I have it on the authority of Mrs Frances B. Ball, widow of the Chaplain who was with Haigh on the last grim morning, that her husband 'loved' him, much as he deplored his heinous crimes.

'Baden* knew him at Dartmoor years before! He had access to the library books, physics, chemistry, Law, etc., which he used a good deal. I *believe*, but not positive, he got some kind of Diploma via a Correspondence College.'

It is ironic to reflect that Haigh used the facilities of Dartmoor's library in order to perfect his knowledge of chemistry so that he would be able to dissolve the bodies of his future victims in acid and then use his prison-acquired knowledge of Law in order to gain possession of their estates. Truly a case of a little knowledge being a dangerous thing.

'Haigh certainly had acquired charm which doubtless he used to camouflage his eventual designs on his unsuspecting victims and was very conceited too, having got away with other crimes,' Mrs Ball continued. 'In the case of Mrs Durand-Deacon, the elderly widow in Onslow Court Hotel—his conceit proved his guilt!'

'*Most positively* Baden spent many hours with Haigh in the condemned cell and was with him an hour on the fatal morning and had Meditation and Prayers for which Haigh thanked Baden.'

I have had access to Haigh's letters to his parents from various prisons and the death cell at Wandsworth, as well as others that he wrote when he was a fire-watcher in London during the blitz. Some of them are reproduced in the following pages.

Dr Noël C. Browne, TD, the brilliant Dublin psychiatrist and

* The Reverend Baden P. H. Ball, Chaplain at Dartmoor and Wandsworth.

former Minister of Health in the Eire government, a man with vast experience of psychopathic patients, renowned for his humane dedication in curing the mentally sick, has been good enough to study these letters as well as the verbatim account of the trial of Haigh. Having done so, he sheds an entirely new light on the character of the Acid Bath Murderer, advancing a theory that may surprise and even shock lawyers as well as members of his own profession, but a theory that I find totally convincing.

Shortly after Haigh had been executed a crime reporter wrote, 'John George Haigh will forever remain an enigma—a many-sided character, baffling even to the doctors who examined him, lawyers and prison officers.'

Thanks to Dr Browne, the character of John George Haigh is no longer an enigma. In his analysis, he has simplified what appeared to be complex, solved what seemed to be a mental jigsaw with a clarity that is both startling and convincing.

John George Haigh became a fire-watcher during the blitz on London, evading any other form of national service, probably because it gave him opportunities for petty villainy and undoubtedly because he enjoyed watching fires. Writing to his parents from gaol, just before his trial for the murder of Mrs Durand-Deacon, he commented, 'Quite a fire in Glasgow! I love fires. I remember the fires during the War. I always thought it a pity they had to be put out; they always fascinated me.'

Dr Noël Browne told me, when I first asked him about Haigh: 'It is possible that he found as much pleasure in killing as he did in watching fires. Given other circumstances and a different upbringing, he might well have become an RAF pilot bombing Dresden and exulting in it. In which case, he could quite easily have gone down in history as a hero instead of a monster.'

Had he not become a multi-murderer Haigh would not have gone down in history at all, except for his somewhat unspectacular niche in the Criminal Records Office. In November 1934 he was sentenced to fifteen months at Leeds Assizes for conspiring to defraud, aiding and abetting a forgery, obtaining money by false pretences, with six other cases taken into account. Three years later, almost to the day, he was sentenced at Surrey Assizes to four years penal servitude for false pretences, twenty-two other cases being taken into consideration. In June, 1941, he received twenty-one months hard labour at London sessions for stealing, among other things, five bunks, sixty yards of curtaining and a refrigerator.

This comparatively minor charge seems to indicate that, for the time being, he had lost confidence in his skill for fraud and forgery, but perhaps circumstances were not propitious. It does make one side of his character apparent, however. The fastidious Haigh, who would not dirty his hands on his own car, was prepared to turn them to anything in order to earn himself a dishonest pound.

Yet it would not be true to say that all his enterprises were fraudulent. A visit to London and the lights of Piccadilly gave him the idea of selling electric news signs to cinemas in the north of England. He succeeded in getting one installed, outside the Majestic Cinema, Leeds. It is ironic that this same electric 'news-reel' was the medium whereby his name first went up in lights—recording his conviction at Leeds Assizes.

Let us take a long and detailed look at the monster who might have been a hero; a new look.

Curtain Raiser

On Sunday, July 17th, 1949, not even the witches of Endor could have invoked more thunder, lightning and rain, the deluge at times being of almost biblical proportions, which was not inappropriate because the most talked about man in the country about to face trial for murder on the following day had been given an Ark to play with when a small boy. The Sabbath calm of the ancient town of Lewes was violated from the matins to evensong by thunder which could have been likened to celestial drumrolls preceding the *pièce de rèsistance* of a spectacularly diabolical tightrope walker. The old place, cradled in the Sussex Downs, had not known a storm like it since Anne of Cleves, the Flanders Mare, had lived nearby. The wonder of it was that the ruins of the Castle survived.

In the history of crime there had never been a more diabolical, more charming, more personally fastidious and agreeable walker of a tightrope than dapper John George Haigh who was in the local prison, apparently quite unconcerned that he might end his days dangling on the end of one of those ropes made by the Southwark firm which incongruously enough also supply marquees for garden parties, the same firm which made the flags for Nelson's immortal signal.

England indeed was expecting that every man called to jury

service at the opening of the Lewes Summer Assizes on the following day would indubitably do his duty.

The meteorological sound and fury was not confined to Sussex. Storms over London had dispersed two thousand dockers who had marched in some industrial demonstration of protest from Canning Town to Trafalgar Square, led by a band of pipers in sodden kilts, their wailing pibroch being a fit accompaniment to the weather. Even some of the stones from Tower Bridge were dislodged by the Tempest.

Yet a Gale Force 10 would not have dispersed the queue of macabre lovers of Grand Guignol which began to form before the bells tolled for evensong in the many-gabled High Street outside Lewes County Hall where on the morrow John George Haigh, erstwhile choirboy and High Altar server, was to stand trial for the murder of an Army officer's widow, Mrs Olive Henrietta Helen Olivia Robarts Durand-Deacon, a woman who believed that Bacon wrote the works of Shakespeare.

Haigh, who had occupied the next table to her at the Onslow Court Hotel in South Kensington, had confessed to murdering her, claiming that she was his ninth victim, and that he had taken a glass of blood from each.

Those who braved the elements all night for the opening of the 1949 Summer Sussex Assizes at Lewes formed as improbable a cross-section of the community as even Haigh's victims. First in the queue was a veteran of the French Foreign Legion, a sixty-two-year-old man from East Grinstead, camp stool under his arm, army surplus waterproof over his shoulders, trousers tucked inside the tops of wellington boots.

'No, the weather doesn't deter me,' he said. 'As an old legionaire I'm accustomed to sleeping rough. Yes, I've heard of Landru. The Bluebeard of Gambais. Tried and executed at Versailles, he was.'

Behind the legionaire was a woman from Eastbourne, primly bespectacled, suitably attired in black, carrying her sandwiches and her knitting in a string bag, rather like those old French ladies who used to sit around the guillotine during the Terror. She told me that she had previously waited all night outside the Old Bailey to get into the public gallery to watch the trial of another infamous murderer, George Neville Heath.

'Some people might think I'm daft,' she told me. 'But I'm interested in these cases.'

Breathing down the lady's neck was a serious young man, a solicitor's clerk. His interest, he claimed, was purely professional. He wanted to get a close-up view of the forensic methods of Sir Hartley Shawcross, KC, MP, Attorney General and leading Counsel for the Crown. One can only hope that his all-night vigil was beneficial to his subsequent career, for the Attorney General's cross-examination of the sole witness called for the defence was nothing short of masterly.

Dr Yellowlees had every reason to regard himself as something of a savant in his profession, a Spilsbury of the psychiatric world and, like that distinguished pathologist, he had become accustomed to juries accepting his expert evidence as gospel, sacrosanct and not to be challenged. He was sixty-one years of age at the time of Haigh's trial. He had been decorated with the Order of the British Empire for his services to medicine. In the 1914–18 War he was a captain in the Royal Army Medical Corps. (Ironically, one of Haigh's victims, Dr Henderson, was also a captain in the RAMC during the 1939–45 War.) Henderson proved to be no great shakes as a doctor, being more of a playboy by inclination, but Dr Yellowlees became Honorary Consulting Physician and Lecturer in Mental Diseases at St Thomas's Hospital, London. He was a leading practitioner of pyschiatric medicine in England.

Therefore, it must have been a surprise for him when his evidence on behalf on Haigh was demolished under the cross-examination of Sir Hartley Shawcross. It was an experience that influenced him to such an extent that he could not resist complaining in a lecture to students, 'Never before or since have I felt that the atmosphere of the court was definitely unfriendly and hostile.'

When I asked him to expand upon his allegation of a 'hostile' court, he wrote to me: 'The trial you refer to took place over 20 years ago. All its horrifying details were duly exploited by a certain type of Sunday newspaper, and I do not believe that any good or desirable purpose could possibly be served by a further book on the subject at the present time.'

I beg to differ. In any case, Dr Yellowlees himself devoted space to the Haigh trial in his own book, *To Define True Madness*, from which he has forbidden me to quote.

'My own personal feeling,' he wrote, 'is very strongly against your making any reference to the contents of the book, and I should be disposed to use any powers that I might possibly have in the matter to prevent this.'

I consulted Lord Shawcross on the allegation of Dr Yellowlees that he had been subjected to an unfriendly and hostile reception in Court. Lord Shawcross replied, 'So far as concerns the remark of Dr Yellowlees, however, I cannot refrain from observing that I saw no sign of antagonism on the part of the Court. He had, however, a very unattractive case.'

I also consulted Mr Justice Christmas Humphreys whose father, Sir Travers Humphreys, was the Judge presiding over the trial of John George Haigh.

Mr Justice Christmas Humphreys wrote to me, 'I know my father's views on the evidence of Dr Yellowlees would never pass the laws of libel if repeated.'

I also happen to know that when the executor for the estate of Haigh's parents showed Dr Yellowlees the letters their son had written from prison and the death cell, asking his advice on what should be done with them, he replied, 'Burn them!'

This advice was tendered over a luncheon table at Grosvenor House, in London.

'It was advice that coming from that exalted source completely staggered me,' said the executor for the modest estate of Haigh's parents. 'And you have been the only person to peruse the Haigh letters since it was given.'

Dr Yellowlees's advice is perhaps surprising from a distinguished man whose professional life had been devoted to alleviating the sicknesses of the mentally deranged, restoring not a few to the paths of normalcy; enjoying the respect and admiration of his colleagues; honoured by his country.

Unlike Dr Yellowlees, Dr Browne found the study of Haigh's letters professionally rewarding and I am grateful to him for his erudite analysis, challenging as it might be.

Therefore, I have no compunction in printing extracts from the letters which Dr Yellowlees would have burned. Why he would have wished them to be consigned to the flames I do not know. They can offend nobody. They are chatty, light-hearted and often trite when intended to be lofty. 'Pathetic' is the word Dr Noël Browne used in describing some of them.

In the queue behind the solicitor's clerk that wet and windy night at Lewes was an art student from faraway Savannah, Georgia, with her cousin and a girl friend.

These three girls had arrived with sleeping bags, blankets and pillows, plus a flask of brandy to sustain them.

Ann said, 'We've come to see what goes on in this country and this is the best way to do it.'

Not one in twenty of those who queued all night would be able to view the proceedings on the morrow, the public gallery having capacity for less than forty people. Although hundreds would be turned away in the morning, people with influence were able to get into the body of the Court. Among them was Robert Montgomery, the American film star and director. One wonders whether he was garnering background for his film *Eye Witness*. Felix Topolski, the artist, also got in to sketch the proceedings for the *Notable British Trials* series.

All over England telephone wires had been blown down, but at Lewes engineers were laying on a special line from Downing Street to the seventeenth-century White Hart Hotel, opposite the Court, in case the Attorney General might be required on matters more important than the fate of John George Haigh. Other lines were being repaired to ensure that the army of reporters, most of them staying at the Crown, would be able to telephone their stories to the newspapers.

Miss Gertrude Charman, supervisor of the Lewes telephone

exchange had engaged extra staff and all the girls had agreed to work overtime.

Ivy Alcorne, the thirty-two-year-old chauffeuse, went to bed early, because in the morning she would be driving the octogenarian Mr Justice Travers Humphreys, the oldest surviving judge in England, from his lodgings to the Court where he would be greeted by a fanfare of trumpets.

Mr Justice Humphreys was sleeping at Antioch House which had been loaned to him by Mr and Mrs Heriot, proprietors of Shelley's Hotel, which had once been a private house belonging to relatives of the poet, a house once visited by Dr Johnson accompanied by Mrs Thrale.

One man who was losing no sleep over the impending trial was John George Haigh himself. He was lodged in the small, ex-naval prison which, during the Crimean War, had housed Russian prisoners of war, on the edge of the Downs and race-horse gallops, a mere couple of furlongs or so from where the old judge was sleeping.

Haigh had written to his parents in a care-free mood, almost as if on holiday, 'Coming down this morning we came through tremendous rain. There were dozens of cars demobilised at Caterham, Godstone and Westerham.

'Of course you don't take the *Daily Express* but had you done so yesterday you would have been amused by the half page they gave me. Biggest attraction to sleepy town of Lewes is J.G.H. Hoteliers and candlemakers expect record custom.

'Judge Humphreys (*sic*) resting during week-end, ready for the case, etc, etc. Loads of drivel ending up with: Haigh last night (*Times*) awaits the car which would take him through the country, etc—and finally which made me hoot with mirth—he has bought himself a brand (*sic*) new suit for the occasion. I'm glad they told me otherwise I wouldn't have known! Also in view of their story I suppose it was my ghost which came down today!'

He told his parents that Lewes was 'a nice county prison'.

The preliminary hearing had been in the Sussex market town of Horsham in the old courthouse overlooked by a stuffed bear outside an inn, photographers perched precariously on the window sills to get pictures of Haigh arriving in his Lovat green suit, smiling like a film star.

The man who had confessed to nine murders, dissolving the bodies of his victims in drums of acid, bought a huge mincer from Gamages to pulverise the bones of two of them, claimed to have drunk their blood as well as his own urine, affected to be quite upset by the behaviour of the morbid sightseers.

'Hundreds of crazy women paying for mobbing the place,' he wrote to his mum and dad. 'Even paying for seats in shop windows.'

Like a pop star who pretends to shun publicity and the adulation of fans, this star criminal was really relishing what he feigned to condemn.

'I was very distressed to read that children and dogs had been trampled on in the mad stampede. I do hope they weren't hurt. What criminal lunatics some women are. Fancy taking children into a crowd like that. Obviously the kiddies wouldn't know what it was all about; they wouldn't be a bit interested and would have been much happier in the fields. And the husbands when they got home and found no lunch were probably contemplating action for divorce.'

Haigh's simulated distress at the mob's morbid behaviour then petered out and he gave vent to his real feelings when describing his journey back from the magistrate's court. One can imagine him chuckling as he wrote, 'I was attached to a fat policeman coming out of court on Friday. He was so anxious to dodge the crowd that instead of waiting for me to get into the car first he jumped in, tripped over the step and fell headlong inside. I of course had to follow. In sorting himself out he got his left leg crossed over his right arm, my right arm underneath him. And that's how we had to go back. If only the press could have seen that! I just howled with laughter all the way to the police station.'

It was a Laurel and Hardy situation.

Could any sane man on trial for his life have penned a letter like that? He concluded it with the words, 'The man who was driving could hardly drive for laughing. I do wish you could have seen it.

'Tata for now,

'Lots of love, Sonnie.'

John George 'Sonnie' Haigh was awakened on the Monday morning, not by the clanging of the prison bell, but by the sounds of the galloping hooves of race-horses. Horses trained by Tom Masson, Matt Feakes, Don Butchers and Harry Hannon. There was a tip going around the prison that the locally trained All Set would win the Glyndebourne Plate. The tobacco barons in the little prison were laying even money in 'snout' on the favourite. They were also making a book on Haigh's chances of escaping the rope. Lewes was a great little prison for punters, Darbie Sabini* having been an inmate there.

Haigh was all set for his star role. He put on his Lovat green suit, carefully knotted his foulard tie of green and red squares, brushed his glossy hair and combed his Hitlerian moustache.

Ivy Alcorne was putting on her dark blue jacket and slacks, black tie and white blouse, to drive the Daimler to pick up Mr Justice Humphreys, a pleasant change from weddings and funerals.

Three hours later, Mr Justice Travers Humphreys was donning his scarlet, ermine-trimmed robe, full-bottom wig, buckled black pumps and white gloves, thus investing himself with the time-honoured regalia essential for the opening of an Assizes. The eighty-two-year-old judge was a stickler for formality, and like Haigh himself, something of a fop on his personal attire. Outside the courts, Mr Justice Travers Humphreys was rarely seen without a black or grey silk topper worn at a jaunty angle, plus butterfly collar and silk bow-tie.

In his youth, this learned judge with a face as wrinkled as an old crab apple, had ridden a penny-farthing bicycle. Nobody

* Once the leader of a race-course gang.

could accuse him of having a penny-farthing mind—although Haigh, of all people, had told his mum and dad that the old judge was 'very stupid' and 'loves playing to the gallery.'

Mr Justice Humphreys had been a member of the Central Criminal Court Bar Mess since 1891 and a Judge since February, 1928, one of the rare instances of a barrister being appointed to such eminence without previously taking silk, *i.e.* becoming either a KC or QC. His great-great-great uncle had been legal adviser briefly to William Corder, the murderer of Maria Marten, the case which inspired what is probably the best known of all stage melodramas, *Murder in the Red Barn.* Old Tod Slaughter toured the halls with it on countless occasions, alternating it with that equally riotous piece '*The Demon Barber of Fleet Street,*' delighting generations of audiences who left the gallery littered with peanut shells and orange peel.

The hundreds of people who lined Lewes High Street on that July morning sucked wafers and ice-cream cornets. The crowd was unprecedented, because the crimes of John George Haigh were more blood-curdling than that of William Corder or the legendary Demon Barber.

Lewes had known sensational trials before—those of Field and Gray, Patrick Mahon, Norman Thorne and others—but nothing like this one. The pavements of the old High Street were so crowded that shopkeepers had difficulty in getting to their premises to unlock them.

Chief Constable Reginald Breffit, standing on the steps of the County Hall, said, 'There are more people here than on Bonfire Night.' (Those people who vociferously campaign for the return of capital punishment might ask themselves why sensational murders since the abolition of the death penalty no longer attract frenzied crowds.)

John George Haigh was the son of Plymouth Brethren parents, an only child born when his mother was in the forties. In his defence, Sir David Maxwell Fyfe was to dwell upon Haigh's strict upbringing.

Haigh was not the only son of strictly religious parents to

make history in the ancient town of Lewes. On his way to the trial at the County Hall, the Acid Bath Murderer was driven past the Bull House where Thomas Paine, author of *The Rights of Man*, the *Age of Reason* and most of Jefferson's *Declaration of Independence*, lodged with a Quaker tobacconist and snuff retailer, eventually marrying the daughter of the house. Her name was Elizabeth and she was twenty years of age, 'pretty enough to attract men of higher rank and greater delicacy.'

Thomas Paine never consummated the marriage. Haigh never made any sexual advances to his numerous girl friends and his own marriage to the daughter of a music hall artiste proved abortive.

Thomas Paine's parents, like Haigh's, were poor, pious and industrious. Paine's mother was thirty-seven years of age before she married and was said to be of a 'sour temper and eccentric'. Paine, like Haigh, was an only child. Paine, like Haigh, was brought up under a 'sense of sin and abhorrence of frivolity'.

Paine's mother was so religious that she refused to milk a cow on Sundays. Haigh's mother would not allow him to play in the park on a Sunday. Haigh's father protested to his schoolmaster for allowing him to read *Treasure Island.*

Thomas Paine, according to W. E. Woodward, his biographer, was the 'godfather of the American revolution' and was responsible for naming that country the United States of America. John George Haigh, who had a similar upbringing, goes down in history as a loathsome murderer, albeit a superficially charming one.

Comparison of the two men is not at all incongruous. Sir David Maxwell Fyfe was to tell the Lewes jury of Haigh's boyhood —'brought up in the most severe surroundings and suddenly changing from that to going to Wakefield Cathedral which at that time was extremely High Church; and, by that change in the formative years of puberty and adolescence, there started in the mind these dreams which were based on a representation of the bleeding Christ, with the blood dripping from his wounds, which the accused has said came into his mind and was the subject of dreams which occurred again and again in his formative years.'

Sir David, in stressing the danger of excessive religious dogma being instilled into the very young and emotionally susceptible, might well have quoted Tom Paine himself.

The author of *The Rights of Man* once wrote, 'I well remember, when about seven or eight years of age, hearing a sermon read by a relative of mine, who was a great devotee of the church, upon the subject of what is called *Redemption by the death of the Son of God.* After the sermon was ended I went into the garden.

'I revolted at the recollection of what I had heard, and thought to myself that it was making God Almighty act like a passionate man, that killed his son when he could not revenge himself any other way; and I was sure a man would be hanged that did such a thing. I could not see for what purpose they preached these sermons.'

Haigh's remains were buried behind the high walls of Wandsworth Prison, but nobody knows where poor Paine's bones are scattered. In order to arouse the social conscience of England to honour one of her greatest sons, Thomas Cobbett journeyed to New Rochelle, USA, dug up Tom Paine's remains and brought them to Liverpool, intending to stage a spectacular, if not a State funeral, but his grisly baggage of bones went astray and history does not record what happened to them.

Shortly after ten-thirty on the morning of July 18th, 1949, Bandsmen Bond and Bland sounded a fanfare on the steps of Lewes County Hall and the frail, octogenarian judge lifted the skirts of his scarlet gown as he stepped out of the hired Daimler, like an old dowager on her way to a ball.

John George Haigh was in one of the cells doing the *Daily Telegraph* puzzle. He took the paper with him up the steps into the dock.

The Clerk of the Assize stood up and intoned, 'John George Haigh, you stand charged that you, on the 18th day of February of this year in this country, murdered Olive Henrietta Helen Olivia

Robarts Durand-Deacon. How say you on this indictment, are you guilty or not guilty?'

In a voice that still held a trace of the soprano of his choirboy days, Haigh replied, 'I plead not guilty.'

The Clerk of the Assize then addressed the jury of eleven men and one woman, thus—'Members of the jury, the prisoner at the Bar stands indicted in the name of John George Haigh for that he, on the 18th day of February of this year in this County murdered Olive Henrietta Helen Olivia Robarts Durand-Deacon. To this indictment he has pleaded not guilty; your charge is to hearken unto the evidence and say whether he be guilty or not guilty.'

The prisoner did not appear to be listening. He had returned to his crossword puzzle, as calm as a commuter on a London train, possibly calmer.

Back in his cell that night he wrote to Mum and Dad up in Leeds, 'Had I not got my *Telegraph* crossword puzzle to amuse me in court today I should have found it very boring, having gone through all the detail before. But interest arose when Sir David began to expound upon the spiritual aspects of the case. As he develops that tomorrow my interest of course will heighten. I have no need to bore you with details of today as you will get that—probably with loads of parsley to adorn the fish—in your papers tomorrow. Ba* was there. May the spirit of Infinity work upon your minds and fortify you and give you solace.

'Lots of love, Sonnie.'

* Barbara Stephens, a Crawley girl and Haigh's constant companion at concerts.

The Little House in Ledger Lane

The most melancholy of the many journeys I made in the footsteps of John George Haigh was the walk I took one raw, wintry afternoon from a little house in Ledger Lane, near Outwood Colliery, to Wakefield Cathedral, a distance of about two miles. It is a bleak road, the skyline gashed by the derelict gallows of executed pitheads, although the air still seems to be impregnated with the coal dust of many yesteryears and redolent of fish and chips. The bay windows of several of the little houses were daubed with whitewash signs announcing 'Frying Tonight'. Melancholy men in 'Andy Capp' caps were exercising whippets. Others had homing pigeons in baskets and I could not help reflecting that any pigeon winging back to this district of its own volition must be a particularly stupid kind of bird. Old women still wore shawls like characters out of *Love on the Dole*. Pakistanis drove past in gaudy cars and the meanest abodes sported television aerials. The melancholy men called their whippets to heel and raised their caps as a funeral cortege went past, the converted Rolls Royce hearse containing enough floral tributes to stock the Berkeley Square windows of Moyses Stevens.

When little 'Sonnie' Haigh used to make this journey every Sunday morning on his way to the cathedral there were tramlines, but he was out and about in his best suit before the first tram left the depot, before the horse-drawn milk cart started on its round. Every Saturday night Mr Haigh set the alarm clock for five o'clock the following day, so that his son, with shining morning face, would be in time for the first Mass at the cathedral, to don crisp white surplice with ruffed collars and cuffs, to sing sweetly on the Cantoria side of the choir. In winter, of course, to serve at the High Altar this small boy would set out in pitch darkness but his heart and his footsteps were light because music was the joy of his life.

He was so gifted musically that at the age of ten he had won a scholarship to Wakefield Cathedral. The puzzling aspect of this is the fact that his parents allowed him to take any part in these highly ritualistic Anglican services.

To Mr and Mrs Haigh, as members of the Plymouth Brethren, the incense, the colour and the grandiose music of High Church services was an anathema.

I tried to imagine what went on in the mind of that neatly clad little boy as he trudged along that bleak road on Sunday mornings, hours before less dutiful and grubbier lads went around stuffing copies of the *Empire News* and the *News of the World* into the letter-boxes of families less sanctimonious than the Haighs.

None of the residents in that somewhat drab area of hard-working, down to well below earth miners could have possibly imagined that the prim and proper Haighs' sweet-voiced little boy would one day make the headlines on the front pages of the sober as well as the lurid newspapers.

Sartorially, he was a Little Lord Fauntleroy among the rougher kids. He was not allowed to play with them because his parents considered they were spiritually and socially superior to their neighbours, despite their own humble origin.

On her death bed after her son had been hanged, the broken-hearted Mrs Haigh said to a friend to whom she entrusted Sonnie's death-cell letters, 'We used to despise the people in the village because we thought we were God's elect. But we were not.'

Molly Lefeburg,* who was Professor Keith Simpson's sec-

* Author of *Murder With a Difference*, Heinemann, 1958.

retary at the time when he exhumed the remains of Mrs Durand-Deacon, wrote 'John and Emily Haigh were Yorkshire people from Altofts. John Haigh, Senior, was a skilled electrical engineer. Proud, genteel and poor, fervently religious, unwordly, honest, diligent. They had been married eleven years before their first and only child was born, the father then being thirty-eight and the mother forty.

'The months of strain Mrs Haigh underwent during her pregnancy were the cause of the mental disease which she alleged her son suffered from, and which she alleged turned him into a criminal.'

Haigh's father, according to Mrs Haigh, was out of work when his son was born and suffered the dire humiliation of having to borrow from his fellow Plymouth Brethren to pay for the expenses incurred, the midwife, cradle, swaddling clothes, napkins, dillwater, additional milk and all the other incidentals incurred in childbirth. There was no dole in those days, no family allowances.

Mrs Haigh said she was 'six months gone' when her husband, through no fault of his own, lost his job. They were living at Stamford, Lincolnshire, which at that time was reputed to have more parish churches than any other town of similar size in England.

John George Haigh was born there in July, 1909, the week of the Flower Show which was described as a 'brilliant success', Lord Exeter winning prizes for his tomatoes, melons, Gentlemen's Button-Holes and Lady's Sprays. Bleriot had flown the Channel from a field near Calais to the vicinity of Dover Castle, Gaumont getting exclusive pictures of the flight.

In Trafalgar Square ten thousand people had protested about the forthcoming visit of the Czar of all the Russias.

Small wonder there was no space in the local papers of Stamford for the birth of a son to an unemployed electrician. Another child destined to be a music lover and to make fame rather than infamy was also born there, Malcolm Sargent, later to be nicknamed 'Flash Harry'. John George Haigh was nicknamed 'Chinky' by his boyhood companions—he had no real friends, not being allowed to play games, but his parents bought him a puppy and pet rabbits.

By this time they had moved from Stamford to Outwood where Mr Haigh had obtained a job as foreman electrician, in the colliery. He was a tall, erect man with a moustache wax-tipped in the old sergeant-major style. The chairs in the front parlour of the little house in Ledger Lane were also straight-backed and well waxed with furniture polish. There was a little organ on which 'Sonnie' first displayed his musical talent, playing only the most solemn, dirge-like hymns, no Verdi's *Requiem Mass*, no Handel's *Messiah*, no Blake's *Jerusalem*, nothing rousing or spiritually stimulating.

Haigh was by no means the only murderer who derived pleasure from playing the organ. George Joseph Smith used to play *Abide With Me* after he had drowned one of his many brides in the Bath. Charlie Peace used to play the organ in a Peckham church.

Norman Thorne, also tried at Lewes, attended Band of Hope meetings with his future victim, Elsie Cameron. Seddon, the poisoner, was a lay preacher. Christie was in a Boy Scout band. Landru sang in a choir. Brodie was a deacon.

Dr Noël Browne is of the firm opinion that religion should not be taught in schools, whether Roman Catholic, Protestant or any other denomination.

'I speak with some authority on this subject as the product of two Catholic schools, one the Marist and one the Christian Brothers. . . .

'We must continue to advocate the complete removal of the religious orders from our schools with their ultimate secularisation. In fact this is now inevitable anyway due partly to the falling off of vocations and also to the nearly pandemic proportions of defections from the religious life throughout the world.

'It is clear too that with growing literacy, greater intellectual sophistication, easier access to higher education, together with the knowledge that lay social workers—nurses, teachers, doctors and many others—do just as valuable and humanitarian service to society as do the religious orders.'

It must be remembered that Haigh was brought up to believe implicitly in the Bible, a saga of slaughter unsurpassed, a holocaust of horror unmitigated, literally to believe in Sodom and Gomorah, Lot's wife, Herod's daughter, Rufus and Esau.

He could recite the goriest passages from the Bible at an age when most children are lisping Goldilocks.

Day in and day out his loving parents told him that the slightest misdemeanour might bring the wrath and vengeance of the Almighty down on his little head. His parents gave him an Ark to play with and religious books at Christmas. When he was naughty his mother punished him by smacking him on the hands with the bristle side of a brush. He said this drew blood which he licked and enjoyed. He also told doctors that he was once locked in a room for two days on bread and water.

Yet his father said, 'John was a good boy and right up to the time he left home he never misbehaved. He got on very well with the other boys and there was nothing wrong with him mentally.'

I would be inclined to the view that there was something indeed wrong with the mentality of a boy who never misbehaved. I have talked to men who were with him at school and the consensus of opinion was that he was unpopular. 'Chinky' is not a very friendly sort of nickname and it is difficult to see how 'he got on very well with the other boys' when he was not allowed to mix with them outside the school or the Cathedral.

Despite the father's assertion that his son never misbehaved, there is no doubt that he was mischievous, which is surely more normal in a boy than being a male Goody Two-Shoes.

A man who was a fellow chorister with young Haigh at Wakefield Cathedral recalled to me how 'Chinky' crept out from his place on all fours, unobserved by any of the officiating clergy or the congregation, found the main electric light switch and plunged that mock-Gothic house of God into utter darkness just when a local dignitary was reading the Lesson on the theme of *And the Lord Said Let There by Light*. The sort of jape one might expect to be played by Miss Richmal Crompton's endearing William rather than a boy destined to become a mass murderer.

A less endearing tale of the young Haigh was told me by a friend of the family.

'A woman in Ledger Lane was on her knees, scrubbing her doorstep, when young Haigh came along. He paused, stamped on one of her hands and ran off, laughing.'

I asked why the unfortunate woman did not complain to Haigh's parents about their 'little angel's' behaviour or administer summary chastisement herself, and my informant explained to me, 'Apart from the fact that the Haighs were aloof and almost unapproachable, it must be remembered that Mr Haigh was foreman electrician at the colliery, the source of employment for most of the residents in Ledger Lane. Jobs were not all that easy to get in those days and if the woman had boxed young Haigh's ears her husband might have found himself out of a job.'

I spoke to Mrs O. M. Adshead-Breckon, an elderly lady who was a Junior School teacher at Wakefield Grammar School when she was Miss Orme.

'J. G. Haigh was in my class,' she said. 'I remember him as a most exemplary pupil with an alert, intelligent face and bright eyes, always immaculately neat and clean, extremely well-behaved and most anxious to please—often ingratiatingly so.'

Mrs Adshead-Breckon was aged 72 when I discussed Haigh with her. She told me she was abroad at the time of his trial and 'it was not until many years later when I saw a photograph of him taken when he was nine years old that I recognised him immediately and felt quite overcome that such a "nice" little boy should end up in such a dreadful way'.

How than can anybody oppose further study of the mind of a murderer? There seems little point in spending millions of pounds on Chairs of Criminology at our universities if we destroy the very documents that are invaluable in our attempts to fathom the mind of a particularly nauseating murderer. It is deplorable to pander to the horrific. It is equally undesirable for us merely to recoil from it and seek no solution.

There is no doubt that John George Haigh looked forward eagerly to his Sundays at the Wakefield Cathedral—full of ecclesiastical pomp, if not Popery, and heady incense. He would spend the entire day in the Cathedral, lingering alone in the aisle between Services, gazing up at the huge gilded figure of the crucified Christ which dominates the High Altar, or seating himself at the console so assiduously that in a short while, still a schoolboy, he was appointed assistant organist.

In contrast to the miserable Sunday evenings he had been forced to spend at the hellfire and brimstone Chapel with his parents in Leeds, it was intoxicating.

'I was excited by the spectacle of priests in their vestments,' he said. 'I gazed with fascination at the blood flowing from the wounds of the larger-than-life Redeemer.'

He continued, 'As I grew up I realised that I was different from other people, and that the way of life in my own home was different to that in others.'

How different it was can be imagined by studying the letters of his father, one in particular written in February, 1899, more than ten years before the birth of his son, ten years after the Jack the Ripper murders.

Not that Haigh's father would have taken any interest in the sordid Jack the Ripper crimes. The Brethren did not read newspapers. The peculiar sect to which Mr and Mrs Haigh belonged had expelled one of the brethren for the misdemeanour of 'railing', which I can only interpret as airing his grievances. Haigh's father wrote to the malcontent:

> Dear Brother in Christ, the brethren have carefully considered your letter addressed to the Assembly in October last.
>
> They do not feel called upon to answer all the questions which you ask, but they desire that the charge of railing was based upon your conduct in going about seeking to justify yourself and thereby condemning your brethren, at the same time manifesting a spirit of contempt and a bitterness of mind.
>
> All this the brethren believe to be railing, and on this charge they were reluctantly compelled to decline fellowship with you;

(and whilst brethren feel that they failed in the manner in which the judgment was arrived at, yet they firmly believe that it, in itself, was right).. The brethren also regret that they cannot at present see any grounds for reconsidering your case.

You may be assured that everyone in fellowship is deeply grieved to see you in your present position, yet we look forward to the time when, through God's grace, you may be restored to the happy fellowships of His people. Then we shall be able whilst witnessing for Him here in this scene to be going on together to that blissful moment when, forever in His own presence, we shall see the end of everything which hinders our full enjoyment of Himself, and when He will see of the travail of His soul and be satisfied.

In conclusion, dear brother, we assure you of our desire for the restoration of your soul. We trust the present unhappy circumstances may result in your deepest spiritual blessing, and that honour may be brought to the Name of our Lord Jesus Christ.

We commend you to God and the Word of His Grace,

And remain yours affectionately in Christ,

(Signed) J. R Haigh

(On behalf of the Saints gathered to the Name of our Lord Jesus Christ)

If the above epistle is not that of a religious maniac then I do not know what amounts to religious mania. One wonders how the son of a father capable of penning such self-righteous balderdash could possibly have had a normal outlook upon life or even death. Sir David Maxwell Fyfe endeavoured to convince the Court that John George Haigh was suffering from a paranoiac defect of reason. He failed. It would have been easier to prove that it was Haigh's pious, wax-moustached father who suffered from paranoiac delusions.

In August, 1901, we find him expelling an entire community of these strange Brethren, self-styled saints, thus:

To the Saints meeting at Beverley Street Room, Attercliffe

Dear Brethren,

On behalf of the Saints gathered to the Lord's name at Pitsmoor, and St Mary's Road, Sheffield, we have to inform you that, having regard to your action in Receiving Mr M— into fellowship, which action has resulted in the forced withdrawal of two brethren from your meeting, and also the fact that you have disregarded, and continue to disregard, the remonstrances of your brethren in other meetings—refusing either to meet them or satisfy their consciences in any way—we are no longer free to commend to you or to receive from you.

We feel distinctly feel that your action is independent in its nature, and therefore opposed to all that goes to make up the fellowship which is owned of God, *i.e.* that to allow such would be to compromise the Lord's name, and, therefore, in faithfulness to Him and love to His people, though, we trust, with true sorrow for yourselves we are compelled to take this course.

If we walk in the light as He is in the light, we have fellowship one with another, and the blood of Jesus Christ, His Son, cleanseth us from all sin. To every one amongst you we would say, 'Let him that nameth the Name of Christ depart from iniquity.'

Your affectionate brethren in Christ . . .

If these documents and others like it had been produced at the Summer Sussex Assizes of 1949 I feel that the jury might have returned a different verdict in the case of the Crown v. John George Haigh.

There is no reason to suppose that Mrs Haigh was not every bit as much a religious crank as her husband. It is a pity that *they* did not receive psychiatric treatment long before the birth of their son.

It is small wonder that their angel-faced little 'Sonnie' became an inveterate liar at a tender age to conceal his misdemeanours from this distinctly odd couple, learned to dissimulate in order to deceive, cultivated a charm that was to become second nature to him, a charm that captivated his victims and the Reverend B. H. Powell, the chaplain who knelt in prayer with him on that fateful morning of August 6th, 1949.

I have before me a copy of the reference given to John George Haigh shortly before he left school. It is dated October 23rd, 1926, the year of the General Strike.

The Grammar School,
Wakefield.

J. G. Haigh has been a pupil here since Sept. 1917 when he entered the Junior School; he has now reached Form VI Lower and will be entering for the School Certificate examination (if he stays at school) in July, 1927.

His character and conduct have always been irreproachable: he is a boy of very pleasant manners and address and I think he will show care and assiduity in such work as he is seeking at the County Hall.

A. J. Spilsbury, Headmaster.

It would appear that the only persons young Haigh failed to charm were his own schoolmates. Perhaps children have more intuition than their elders?

For years little 'Sonnie' had been forging the signatures of his various teachers with such expertise that they themselves did not realise what their 'pleasant-mannered' pupil was up to, although there is no suggestion that the above reference is forged. However, this gift of forgery did enable Haigh to carry out a number of impudent frauds later in life. This raises an important question if we are to attempt to fathom the labyrinthine workings of his mind.

Skilled forgers are rare in the underworld. They can obtain rich pickings without much risk to themselves. The system is for letter-box thieves, pickpockets and handbag riflers to steal cheque books and a specimen of the victim's handwriting and signature.

The thief then goes to the forger and asks him or her (some of the most adept are women) to forge a sizeable cheque. The forger gets fifty per cent of the illicit proceeds and runs no risk. It is the 'dropper'—the person who presents the cheque at the bank or elsewhere—who takes the risk. (Credit cards now make it an even more profitable occupation.)

John George Haigh could have derived ill-gotten gains from forgery alone. Why then did he have to murder for money? Could it be that he actually enjoyed murdering?

On the other hand, 'kite droppers' usually work in teams. Possibly the denizens of the seamier fringes of the underworld did not trust John George Haigh. Perhaps he did not trust them.

It was said at Haigh's trial that 'the solitary schoolboy becomes the potential paranoiac'. The solitary schoolboy can also become the solitary criminal, the man who 'goes it alone' in his unlawful deeds. Any detective will agree that it is this type of malefactor who is most difficult to apprehend because he has no associates ready to inform on him at the drop of a hat—or more likely the 'dropsy', *i.e.*, a bribe. The overworked phrase 'honour among thieves' is very much a figment of uninformed imagination. Every criminal is a potential Judas and not necessarily for thirty pieces of silver.

On the 23rd of October, 1926, the Reverend Canon W. A. Macleod, M.A., Vicar of Wakefield Cathedral, wrote of the teenage Haigh, 'I hereby certify that I have known John George Haigh for the past ten years. He is a smart, polite, intelligent boy and has had a good education. He has an excellent character and his home environment is good.

'I have every confidence in recommending him, feeling that he will give satisfaction to all he comes in contact with.'

Apart from the fact that the Reverend Canon Macleod's grammar was not all that impeccable, Haigh's ecclesiastical as well as lay teachers must have been woefully distressed by the subsequent career of their exemplary pupil, his gruesome deeds and equally gruesome end. So much so that when I called on one of them, the Reverend W. E. Plumbridge, at his house, he shut the door in my face. He did not wish to discuss the polite, intelligent little boy whose voice had soared so sweetly into the incense-laden air of Wakefield Cathedral.

I found Mr E. M. Pick more helpful in the rather different atmosphere of his Wakefield Steam Laundry. He was at junior school with Haigh and also a pupil of Mrs Adshead-Breckon, 'a greatly esteemed and well remembered friend of long standing'.

Clouds of steam swirling outside his office where buxom laundry girls were putting sheets through rollers and singing cheerfully, he recollected, 'Haigh was known as "Chinky" because of his narrow eyes.

'I felt rather sorry for him because the other kids teased him on account of the fact that he always wore a small bow-tie and tried so obviously to behave like a little gentleman, which he wasn't.

'He didn't know how to behave with other children—believing himself to be socially and spiritually superior, a feeling obviously instilled into him by his well-meaning but misguided parents.'

It was Mr Pick who suggested that I should see Mr Henry Whitton, of Ashley Avenue, Wakefield. Mr and Mrs Whitton believe that Haigh intended them to be his next victims.

'Haigh's method of murder was all his own,' said Mrs Whitton. 'He would scan the death columns of the newspapers to find people who might have left money.

'Then he would write a letter of sympathy to the relatives to soften them up. In 1949 my husband's father died and soon afterwards a letter arrived signed "John George Haigh".

'This was odd because although we had known Haigh slightly when a boy we had never had any touch with him for more than twenty years.

'One day I was carrying my blazer over my arm when he came up behind me and snatched it away.

'Then he caught hold of my arm and threw my blazer right into the railway track. He was still holding me when he said "There is an express coming and it will run you over and cut you into little pieces and there will be blood all over the place."

'I was terrified but I ran into the middle of the line, snatched the blazer and ran home crying. I would not tell my mother anything but next day I refused to go to school. I got a good hiding and then the whole story came out.

'My mother went straight to the headmistress and after that it was arranged that he would never be let out of school until I had got a fair way away. I was also given a bodyguard of little boys to protect me.'

When it became known that I was in the Leeds and Wakefield area investigating the early life of Haigh the *Yorkshire Post* was inundated with telephone calls from people who had experiences to relate similar to that of Mrs Whitton. Among them was Mrs Joyce Hellar of Jenkin Road, Horbury, who claimed that she was probably the first subject of his fantasies.

'I was five and he was six,' she said. 'He always used to follow me home from the kindergarten where we were both pupils.'

I keep a less than open mind about these stories. If they are true I find it difficult to reconcile them with the references of exemplary behaviour supplied by Haigh's teachers. I am not suggesting that the anecdotes are invented, but memories of childhood experiences can be illusory.

On the other hand, I can believe the story of Mr Henry Whitton, who sang with Haigh in the choir at Wakefield Cathedral.

'Haigh was fond of a prank and would try anything on,' Mr Whitton said.

'In choir practices he used to dress up as a ghost and appear out of the crypt in the gloom of the Cathedral. It scared us out of our wits.'

This, to me, has the ring of truth. Stories of him following and frightening little girls of his own approximate age are not convincing. One thing was made abundantly clear at Haigh's trial was that he behaved perfectly correctly towards his girl friends—and he had a number of very attractive girl friends—but the friendships really were platonic and he derived his greatest joy in feminine company by taking the girl to concerts of classical music, about which he was most knowledgeable. Oddly enough, he would sometimes take the girl of his choice to Madame Tussaud's where eventually his own effigy was destined to go on display in the Chamber of Horrors.

In a top floor flat of Queenswood Heights, Headingley, overlooking Leeds, I talked to Miss Nan Rigby, who was Haigh's fifteen shillings a week typist more than twenty-five years ago when she was just eighteen. Still an attractive woman, she must have been even more so when she worked for Haigh in his dry-cleaning business.

Miss Rigby talked to me frankly about Haigh over drinks which she lavishly dispensed.

'Oh, he was one of the lads of the village, if you get my meaning, a real smartie-pants with glossy hair and a red sports car of which he was inordinately proud, although he would never soil his own hands in cleaning it.

'He nearly always wore chamois gloves, anyway, and looked as if he had just been through a dry-cleaner himself. I didn't realise at the time he was bent on trying to "take *people* to the cleaners", rather than clothes.

'He always behaved perfectly correctly towards me and never made any sexual suggestions or advances. I got the impression that he was more interested in motor cars than girls.

'Then, one day in 1936, the bailiffs or hire-purchase people came in and took all the office furniture away, including the type-writer.

'I was left sitting on the floor with the letters I had been typing. There seemed no point in staying, so I put on my hat and coat and left. I never saw Haigh again or even bothered to ask him for my last week's fifteen-bob wages.

'Oh, yes, George was a star turn, no doubt about that.'

Almost every adult in Wakefield has heard of John George Haigh. Not one in a hundred knows anything about George Gissing, the chemist's son who was born at 30 Westgate, not far from the Cathedral which has a plaque commemorating the founder of the Tootal family of tie and hankie fame.

There is a plaque over the chemist's shop in Westgate, now a Boots, to George Gissing who wrote that sad tale of Victorian times, *The Private Papers of Henry Ryecroft*. The private papers of John George Haigh, despite his apparent bland indifference to the enormity of his crimes and his own dreadful end less than a month after his fortieth birthday, are an even more tragic chronicle of our own times. It is our duty to try to comprehend rather than recoil, to endeavour to understand how a child can grow into a smirking monster, almost exulting in his own awful deeds, because unless we endeavour to understand how it can come about, rather than taking the kids to the Chamber of Horrors as a treat, then we must each one of us share some particle of the guilt.

'Dear Mum and Dad'

It is not for me to moralise, but merely to present the facts, making sure as far as is humanly possible that the facts are indeed facts and not wild surmise, nor hazy recollections of persons trying to recall what happened either in their childhood or their dotage. Day in and day out, witnesses in the criminal and civil courts of this country raise their right hands and swear by the Almighty God that the evidence they are about to give shall be the truth, the whole truth and nothing but the truth.

This solemn oath is ludicrous, because even an impartial witness is incapable of telling the truth, the whole truth and nothing but the truth concerning an event or events that happened the day before yesterday, let alone five, ten or twenty years previously. He or she might conscientiously endeavour to do so, but it is an impossible task.

As an ex-crime reporter I know that every sensational crime story lets loose as many red herrings as may be found in a barrel in Hessell Street market. Every detective will confirm this. Thousands of man-hours are wasted every year in the police forces of the country by good citizens supplying information which they believe to be correct, but which proves after diligent probing to be erroneous.

When Mrs Durand-Deacon disappeared from the Onslow

Court Hotel police forces throughout the country received hundreds of calls from people who imagined they had seen her. Every call had to be checked. Only one man—her murderer—knew that this lady of independent means would never be seen again. He wrote from the hotel:

Dear Mum and Dad, Mrs D. D. has not returned and the Sunday newspapers are full of the most exciting stories imaginable. They are digging up chalk pits looking for her body and all sorts of things. Then a mystery telephone call came through to the hotel last night. Somebody rang up to say they had seen her (or been with her) last Sunday—2 days after she had disappeared. The *Pictorial* speaks of the dapper young Mr Haigh and the *Despatch* of the handsome 35-year-old Mr Haigh. Which kindness rather surprised me since I would give them no information and referred them to the police station. Life was rather a nightmare yesterday, the place was absolutely besieged by reporters and Robbie (manageress and I) spent our time dodging them.

It is sure to turn out to be a most exciting case. If you want excitement come to O.C.H!

My cough has gone now. May gave me some stuff called FAMEL. It is exceptionally good although it is the most revolting stuff to take that I have ever known. Tastes of creosote. Has aconite in it. . . .

Only five days previously he had written to Mum and Dad:

What do you think is the latest excitement? Mrs D. D. has disappeared—or so it is thought. Nobody knows where she is and she has not been seen since Friday when she was going to meet me but didn't turn up. Of course, she can have gone to some relations somewhere & not told anyone. But because that was unusual of her it has naturally led to all sorts of wonderful rumours. A spot of scandal is real bread and butter in this place!

I heard from Madge yesterday. She has arrived in Melbourne and had a nice trip and likes the place she has gone to.

I think everybody else is much the same. Mrs Stephens has had flu this last week, and has been in bed. There is a lot of it about. . . . Lots of love, Sonnie.

Haigh had not one shred of pity for any of his victims, any more than his sanctimonious parents had for the 'offenders' and 'railers' they dismissed so autocratically from their weird religious sect. In fact, after his arrest, he told another prisoner that Mrs Durand-Deacon 'should have been pushing up daisies years ago'.

In his statement made to Detective-Inspector Albert Webb at Chelsea Police Station on February 28th, 1949, he described Mrs D-D. as 'a confounded nuisance' on account of her weight and size when he dissolved her body in a drum of sulphuric acid.

'I laid the barrel down lengthwise on the floor and with a minimum of effort pushed the head and shoulders into the barrel. I then tipped the barrel up by placing my feet on the forward edge and grasping the top of the barrel with my gloved hands. By throwing my weight backwards the barrel containing the body rocked to a vertical position fairly easily and I found I could raise a 15-stone body without difficulty. You may think that a 40 gallon drum standing only 4 ft. high would be too small for such a body, but my experiments showed that as the drums tipped, the body slumped down to the shoulders and the legs disappeared below the surface of the drum. I then donned the rest of my equipment, for I had found it necessary to protect myself from the acid. I had a rubber mackintosh which I kept specially for this purpose, rubber gloves, a gas mask to protect myself from the acid fumes, a rubber apron and rubber boots, such as I had seen referred to in a case that occurred in America a good many years ago. As I have said, the question of getting the right amount of acid into the oil drum was only learnt by experience. Whether a person was thin or fat made a considerable difference and there were occasions when I had far too much acid in the drum, even by the stirrup pump method of adding to it after the body was inside. Thin people were much more easily disposed of, for I found fat most difficult to dissolve. For this reason Mrs Durand-Deacon was a confounded nuisance—far more trouble than any of the others. She simply would not disappear and next day when I expected her body to be entirely dissolved I found a large piece of buttock floating on top of the sludge and grease that was the rest of her. I emptied off the grease and put in fresh acid, expecting that the next day to see the dissolution complete as in previous cases. She simply would not go and there were still some parts left, though quite unrecognisable for what they were, when I emptied the sludge onto a rubbish heap outside the shed and threw the drum carelessly among other scrap iron and other drums that had been used on many occasions.'

No wonder that even an experienced police officer like Detective-Inspector Webb said, 'You have made my stomach turn over. Do you really mean what you say?'

Haigh shrugged, saying complacently that his acid bath method of disposing of a body was 'far more satisfactory than the ghoulish practice of a funeral'.

He was every bit as cold-blooded as George Joseph Smith, the Brides in the Bath murderer, who used to say laconically, 'When they are dead they are dead.'

Haigh did not complete his statement until one o'clock the following morning. On the 24th of March, 1949, he writes, from Prison:

> Dear Mum and Dad, As you say this will be a big case: in fact, I think the biggest case in British history, from so many angles. When before has it been known for a newspaper to have been hauled before the Law Lords to answer a charge of Contempt of Court. What I am going to say now is very difficult to explain. Nobody would understand it. The Pharisees of today least of all. I have had two of them to see me. The C/E Chaplain whose philosophical outlook is useless. No man who represents a church with such a diversity of contradictory opinions could hope to understand. He's got no base upon which to work. The Wesleyan who came at Donald's request was a more hopeful

subject. But both are terribly tiring. Both are escapists from a sphere of reality. Take away their stipend and what would they be: not as Paul who made tents and still did his good work so that men should not say he was dependent on the brethren.

Haigh's mention of a newspaper being hauled before the Law Lords referred to the case of *Rex* v Silvester Bolam and Daily Mirror Newspapers Limited. Ex parte Haigh, for contempt of Court. It was alleged that on March 4th, 1949, the *Daily Mirror* headlined a story on its front page VAMPIRE—A MAN HELD. The story, which carried over onto the back page, began *The Vampire Killer will never strike again. He is safely behind bars, powerless to lure his victims to a hideous death.* On the previous day the same newspaper had splashed the headline *Vampire Horror in Notting Hill,* referring to the disappearance of Dr and Mrs Henderson as well as that of the McSwan family. On the same page was a photograph of Haigh leaving Horsham Magistrate's Court after he had been charged with the murder of Mrs Durand-Deacon.

The *Daily Mirror* had seen fit to disregard the confidential memo to newspaper editors, dated March the 3rd, 1949: 'A report has been published today that New Scotland Yard is investigating a case in which a vampire murderer drinks his victim's blood. The only statement on this matter which has been made to the Police is now *sub judice*.'

This was in the days when the *Mirror* followed a 'Publish and Be Damned' policy—echoing the historic phrase of the Duke of Wellington to Harriet Wilson when she thought to intimidate—or possibly blackmail—him by writing memoirs of her love affairs.

Mr Silvester Bolam, editor of the *Daily Mirror*, appeared before the Lord Chief Justice, then Lord Goddard, Mr Justice Humphreys and Mr Justice Birkett in the King's Bench Division of the Royal Courts of Justice on the 25th of March, 1949.

'In the long history of this class of case there has, in the opinion of this Court, never been a case approaching such gravity as this one of such a scandalous and wicked character,' said the late Lord

Goddard. 'It is of the utmost importance that this Court should vindicate the common principles of justice and in the public interest see that condign punishment is meted out to persons guilty of such conduct....

'The Court has taken the view that there must be severe punishment in this case.' The Lord Chief Justice then addressed the defendant, a thin, bespectacled and somewhat prosaic figure as he faced the bench.

'Silvester Bolam, a writ of attachment will issue against you; you will be taken into the custody of the tipstaff and you will be committed to Brixton Prison for a term of three calendar months.

'The newspaper, Daily Mirror Newspapers, Ltd., will be fined ten thousand pounds and ordered to pay the costs of these proceedings. The money is to be paid to the Master of the Crown Office by twelve o'clock on Monday; otherwise writs of sequestration and *scire facias* will be delivered to the Sheriffs of the City of London.'

It would be untrue to suggest that Fleet Street was appalled by the sentence and fine. In *El Vino's* on the following Monday all sorts of hilarious stories were circulating, one of the most improbable being that the *Mirror* just hadn't got ten thousand smackers, plus costs, in the kitty, and that the management had to borrow it from the *Daily Express*, and that the Beaver had asked, 'What security can they offer? Cecil King's head?'

I discussed the matter many years later with that indiscreet diarist, Mr King, *after* his customary lunch at Claridge's, and he was still smouldering at the recollection.

'Why did they pick on us?' he pontificated. '*The Times* and *Daily Mail* were just as much in contempt of Court. The Law Lords picked on the *Mirror* as a whipping boy.'

I have no doubt that Mr Cecil King has kept a record of our conversation, but the answer to his question is that the Law Lords did not pick on the *Daily Mirror*. The proceedings were not undertaken by the Director of Public Prosecutions, but by a private individual, namely John George Haigh.

Small wonder that he was elated. 'Dear Mum and Dad,' he wrote. 'I should think the result of the *Mirror* case will have staggered you as much as it did me. I just couldn't believe it. Goddard certainly spared no pains in telling them what he thought of them. The only man who will really be happy about it will be old Cripps who will collect £10,000 for his budget which he didn't expect.'

I knew Silvester ('Bish') Bolam. For the editor of a tabloid, he had a childish hobby. This little man with a squeaky voice used to go home and cut out fret-saw puzzles after a day's work headlining the more lurid and fretful puzzles of other people's lives. He was not, I understand, the most popular inmate of Brixton Prison.

I have heard unconfirmed reports that he enjoyed privileges to which he was not entitled, that he got boxes of fifty cigarettes and never gave as much as a 'dog end' away in a place where tobacco is as gold dust. Fellow prisoners even alleged that he was allowed out at night, a chauffeur-driven car picking him up and delivering back at midnight, but I have been unable to obtain any official confirmation of such irregularities.

I have had an equally unconfirmed report—this one from a Scotland Yard detective—that the police themselves put Haigh up to the idea of 'confessing' that he had drunk the blood of his victims, a feat pathologically doubtful, in order to give the impression that he was indeed insane and thus escape the hangman's rope.

I prefer Detective-Inspector Albert Webb's account, who said that when he was alone with Haigh the latter asked, 'Tell me, frankly, what are the chances of anyone being released from Broadmoor?'

Webb then said, 'I cannot discuss that sort of thing with you.'

Haigh then replied, 'Well, if I told you the truth, you would not believe me; it sounds too fantastic for belief.'

Detective-Inspector Webb then gave him the formal caution to the effect that anything he said would be taken down in writing and might be used in evidence at his trial.

Haigh then said, 'I understand all that. I will tell you all about it. Mrs Durand-Deacon no longer exists. She has disappeared completely and no trace of her can ever be found again.'

'What happened to her?' the detective asked.

'I have destroyed her with acid,' Haigh answered. 'You will find the sludge which remains at Leopold Road. Every trace has gone. How can you prove murder if there is no body?'

There was no body, it is true, but there were the remains of one. When Dr Cedric Keith Simpson, pathologist at Guy's Hospital, went to Giles Yard, Leopold Road, Crawley, he found blood stains below the windows of a workshop which was little more than a shed.

Sifting the soil found outside the workshop, Keith Simpson also discovered a set of upper and lower dentures which Helen Patricia Mayo, of New Cavendish Street, London, a dental surgeon, would later identify as having been made for Mrs Durand-Deacon.

Dr Keith Simpson also found the handle of a red plastic handbag, a lipstick container, some gallstones and other bony particles of a human body. The pathologist came to the conclusion that a partly preserved bone of the hip girdle had sex characteristics denoting that it was female. It showed signs of senile change and was that of an elderly woman.

While total immersion of a body in a concentration of sulphuric acid will dissolve it in a few days, gallstones and human fat would resist erosion by acid, as would certain plastics like dentures and the handle of the handbag.

In his book, *The Reluctant Cop*, Detective-Inspector Webb, who later became Detective-Superintendent, described Haigh as the most accomplished criminal he had ever met, 'perhaps the greatest of the century'.

While I cannot agree with this dubious eulogy, I would be inclined to put Haigh in the top ten of unmitigated liars, but then he began to lie as soon as he could toddle. Is it too far-fetched to apportion the blame for this on his puritanical parents? Most children tell an occasional 'fib', but young Haigh had to develop it into a fine art in order to avoid the disapproval of his parents. So he learned to lie as glibly as he learned to forge the signatures of his school teachers.

He lied after in his letters as is all too apparent in many of them. As Mr Justice Humphreys was to say in his summing-up, 'This man is utterly and completely unreliable.'

I regret to reveal, however, that those two pillars of rectitude, Haigh's dearest Mum and Dad, were not exactly the exemplars of truth when discussing their only child. I have quoted from Molly Lefeburg's book in which she describes how Mr Haigh was unemployed during his wife's pregnancy and the months of strain she underwent were the cause of 'the mental disease which she alleged her son suffered from, and which she alleged turned him into a criminal'.

It would perhaps be charitable to assume that Mrs Haigh's memory was at fault when she recounted this tale of hardship. After all, she was in her eighties when her son was on trial for the murder of Mrs Durand-Deacon.

I have incontrovertible proof that Mr Haigh, senior was in a comparatively good job during his wife's pregnancy and that he did not lose it until some five months after little John George was born.

The proof before me is a copy of a reference from Mr J. Edmundson, manager of the Urban Electric Supply Co. Ltd., of Wharf Road, Stamford. It is dated December 11th, 1909, and reads:

> This is to certify that Mr J. Haigh has been on our staff for 6 years having held the position of Station Superintendent at our Stamford and Grantham Works. He is responsible for the erection, running and repairs of the whole plant at these places. He is a capable Engineer having successfully erected 1,000 KW of direct current machinery including Watertube Boilers, High Speed Engines, Dynamos, Switchboards and Batteries.
>
> He is a good organiser, and can be relied upon to look after his department in every way, paying strict attention to economical

working, and our cost sheet shows a considerable improvement as the result of his careful supervision. The satisfactory manner in which he has carried out his duties gives us every confidence in recommending him for a higher position than he has occupied with us, and we are certain that his Electrical and Mechanical knowledge will enable him to give entire satisfaction and his personal character eminently fits him for a position of trust. The reason he is leaving us is due to the completion of both stations, and our desire to reduce the standing costs. We shall, therefore, be pleased to hear of his success in obtaining a better and more lucrative berth.

No man could expect a more glowing reference than that and it is difficult to imagine such a model employee being unemployed for long. He wasn't.

I have before me the copy of another reference in regard to Haigh, senior. It is from the Lofthouse Colliery, Ltd, near Wakefield. It is dated August 29th, 1935:

> I have much pleasure in stating that Mr J. R. Haigh of Outwood, near Wakefield, has been employed as Engineer for the above Company for 26 years. During the whole of that time he has had exceptional opportunities for acquiring a good practical knowledge of pit-work; of the equipment of collieries, of tactfully dealing with workmen and others.
>
> He is a man of earnest purpose, much pertinacity, ability and discretion and his personal character is irreproachable.
>
> I have every confidence in recommending Mr Haigh to your consideration and if he is successful I know he will do all he can to justify your selection.

So Haigh's father must have started work with the Outwood Colliery almost immediately after leaving the Stamford Urban Electric. In fact, it seems to me, that Haigh, senior, was rarely, if ever, unemployed.

Going back even further, to July, 1902, seven years before 'Sonnie's' birth, we find Mr J. R. Haigh leaving the employment of the Sheffield Corporation Electrical Supply Department, where he was Foreman Fitter, 'with a view to bettering his position.'

So much then for the sob story of Haigh's parents being poverty-stricken. So much for the legend of his mother suffering mental anguish as well as physical in her labour because of the social stigma of having to borrow from the neighbours to pay for the swaddling clothes and the cradle. The Haigh's were better off than most of their neighbours and whatever birth pangs Mrs Haigh suffered were certainly not financial. Could this strait-laced old lady have been as convincing a liar in her eighties as her son was from the day he started to prattle until he was hanged by the neck until dead? Did he, in fact, learn to lie at his mother's knee?

He always spoke of her as 'an angel' and throughout his life he wore double-heeled socks which she knitted for him.

He was furious with the prison laundry for losing some of the socks his Mum had knitted for him, telling her that he was 'in a militant mood' about it, complaining to the Governor.

'He was more concerned about those bloody socks than his own neck,' a Brixton Prison officer told me.

It would certainly appear to be so, judging from Haigh's letters on the subject:

> Dear Mum and Dad,
> Still coping with sock situation which is very belaboured owing to the understandably restricted facilities for dealing with same. Outside I would be round at the doorstep kicking up merry delight. No I don't think you need send another pair to go on with as you know I always used to send them with great misgiving wondering whether I should see them again: such wonderful pieces of handicraft that everyone used to remark about. I was livid when they didn't return here. . . .

Later, he writes on the same theme:

> Dear Mum and Dad, You will be pleased to hear that I have retrieved two of the pairs of socks which went astray at the laundry. We have switched over now to the laundry which did my work at the Onslow Court. The local one was just beyond

coping with. There's always a snag about everything these days—and in this case it is that they don't collect in this area*—I'm not surprised. No self respecting laundry would. . . .

Somewhat mollified by getting his socks back, Haigh then permits himself to reveal a little nostalgia for the old homestead, although one questions whether he really means it, or cares a hoot about the little local church when he writes, 'There is no question about would I like to hear the little parish clock chime. I do hear it chime. You see it actually exists as far as I am concerned; I can hear it. I can see it.'

Three days later we find him writing:

Dearest Mum and Dad,

I am going to send you a copy of *The People* which I don't suppose you get. It contains a remarkably good article about Princess Margaret. A beautiful photograph of her in Italy. If the press had confined themselves to such photographs of her holiday there would have been some sense in it. Some of the anecdotes recounted therein are very amusing and just like what Nigel told us after he'd been to Buck House painting the dogs. I love the one about the shaving. And the bit about 'Not before the Minister, Margaret' made me hoot with mirth. You'll probably think it funny as it stands; but I've a very good idea what she sang—having seen the reports of the shows that she has seen—so of course that makes it much better! Barbara expected that she had played a Saucey thing too. It is a song from 'Annie Get Your Gun' entitled 'Doing What Comes Naturally.'

Then this enigmatic man, a self-confessed mass murderer, allegedly a drinker of his victims' blood and of his own urine, adds, 'Did you see Barborelli (*sic*) was in the Honours list? Good egg!'

Good egg, indeed! What a Bertie Woosterish remark to be penned on prison writing paper by a murderer more strange than

* Brixton.

any in fiction, more polite and even more improbable than any character in an Agatha Christie play!

There is one aspect of Haigh's personality that we can be quite certain about. His passion in life was music. Moreover, he was knowledgeable on the subject, and musicians of high standing concert pianists and violinists of renown were among his friends. One even wanted to take a grand piano into the prison and play for him.

Albert Ferber wrote to him on the 16th of May, 1949:

> Dear Mr Haigh, A few nights ago I dined with the F—s and we talked a lot about you, your ears must have been ringing.
>
> I must tell you quite sincerely how deeply sorry I am about all that has happened to you since I saw you last. I can't remember when it was, I believe at one of my concerts at the Wigmore Hall? I have just given another one. I know how happy the F's would have been if they could have brought you along too. I wonder how one could arrange that I could come and play to you. I remember Wandsworth prison used to arrange concerts at which I played, but I don't know about Brixton regulations. They wouldn't allow a piano in privately, I am sure, but perhaps there are possibilities of a concert in some hall or whatever they have? If there is anything I could do for you, I should be happy.
>
> My best and sincere wishes are with you,
>
> Albert Ferber.

What *is* one to make of Haigh, who could commit such loathsome crimes without a qualm and yet inspire genuine affection and esteem in the hearts of people of sensitivity and culture?

Today, Albert Ferber realises that he too might have been numbered among Haigh's victims.

'I did not know him very well,' the concert pianist wrote to me. 'I met him about half a dozen times and he regularly came to my recitals.

'I don't feel he was so much of a complex character, but a

schizophrenic, with two quite simple and straightforward personalities. (Of course, I knew only one side.) I don't know how often he asked me to go and see him at his flat. And something in me always said "no" and I never went and felt rather unkind. Of course, later I was relieved I never went, or I might not now write this letter!'

No more apposite illustration of Haigh's dual character can be found than in another somewhat banal letter to his parents, shortly before being released from his first prison sentence. In this, the future Acid Bath Murderer propagates pacifism, but at the same time reveals a pre-occupation with death, a state of mind not normal in a young man; at least, not normal in the type of young man one associates with kid gloves and smart motorcars.

'We did however observe the service of remembrance on the 11th,' he writes from prison. 'It was very beautiful in its magnificent simplicity. I was led to think of that verse in the book of Macabees: "It is a good and wholesome thing to think of the dead." One could not help thinking at the same time of course of the wretchedness of warfare. Offensive war is utterly unjust and immoral. Quite inconsistent with the theoretical principles of any country calling itself Christian. No condition can ever justify it. But nevertheless a Defensive war can be justified since it may be necessary in the last resort to defend just rights. To pray for peace in the presence of war and on our own decision for rearmament seems almost hypocritical. But as sensible Christians I suppose we can have no other views than peace is the most desirable state for the world. But what many of our statesmen seem to overlook is the fact peace has its price and like all other good things it demands its sacrifices. It is easy to blame Italy for she has made mistakes amounting to folly. In my opinion she has a good case against Abyssinia but did not present it until hostilities were due to commence. . . . There can be no real peace until that great day when the great King of Peace shall return with thousands of his redeemed Saints to subdue the earth, and when all will be in the light: "They saw Jesus only" and "There was a lamb as it had been slain." . . .'

This strange young man then concludes on a more personal note, revealing—or affecting—an intention to turn over a new leaf.

'... this may be my last letter before our reuniting. Then "O What joy and happiness there." I will therefore take this opportunity of reminding you of my goodly intentions. I don't feel like saying a great deal about it. I can perhaps sum it up in this: that I really do intend to make up to you for the past when I come out. I am enjoined by that verse: "Cast your net to right side" and again "The angel stood at the right side of the Altar."

'Please reiterate my thanks to Arthur for his unremitting fidelity. The beautiful flowers which I receive weekly and which give such inexpressible pleasure are a monument to his constancy. I shall not forget it.

'My love now to you all, G.'*

Can any medical man, any lawyer cross his heart and say that John George Haigh was completely sane?

Writing about himself to his Mum and Dad he admits.

I have a reputation for fraud and forgery. But at least I'm honest about it, where they† make an easy living under the cloak of religion. I can only laugh at them. Or I should say I can't take them seriously.

Even you will not understand [he continues]. That's the worst of it nobody does understand me—not that I try to make them: it takes too long to get to know a person and strangers are such fools. But at least you may partly understand—or will you? I don't know. Our philosophers have diverged during the last few years. No one could convince you that you are wrong and no one can convince me that I am—although I have my moments of doubt: these are usually set right, however, by the most extraordinary acts of fate: We have this in common, which I hope may help towards an understanding. We have both a belief in a supreme force. Each thesis runs parallel with the other with different orientations and different perceptions.

* In most cases Haigh signed letters to his parents 'Sonnie.'

† Prison chaplains.

But there we come to a deadlock. You *know* you are right. I *know* that I am. Poor little Ba; that was always a stumbling block to her. She used to go mad sometimes. 'You're always right and what infuriates me is that you know you are: I wish to goodness you'd be wrong sometimes.'

I always remember when Pat fought the bulldog. Everybody was scared and wouldn't touch them. And when I went over to separate them everybody cried me off. Frankly, I was petrified but (a) I wasn't going to admit it (b) I shouldn't get bitten, even though I put my hand in Pat's mouth and pulled him off by his bottom jaw.

Ba said 'I wish to God I had bitten you: you wouldn't have been so sure then. But you're always right, aren't you?'

The fact that I didn't get bitten of course proves that I was right and fortifies me in my belief.

The Medical Officer may understand it though I doubt it. He will get nearer to doing so than any person. We've had a chat already but of course its very difficult talking to strangers. One has to get through to people first. I shall see him more than once whilst I am here and perhaps we may get over the reserve. We shall see if he sees me often enough. Although without the same metaphysical experience he's going to find it hard to understand. You have had experiences of your own which have confirmed your beliefs. The same experiences did not have the same effect on me. The glory in tribulation has a totally different effect on us. Whereas it stimulates you it depresses me. So that my experiences during the past few years have been such as to establish my convictions.

There is a power outside oneself, which leads one on and on and to drink of the river of life is to experience more completely the fulness of life. This doctor here is very good in that he gives one the impression that he is understanding: but as I say we have so far only had a cursory skate around the whole idea.

Callous as a corkscrew and just as straight, Haigh rarely shows any signs of the depression he alleges tribulation brings upon him. It is hard to believe, in fact, that he regarded his trial for murder as tribulation. Nearly all his letters are buoyant as if he is enjoying being 'the star turn' in the macabre proceedings, although sometimes he confesses to boredom but only as an actor might be when hearing the same lines constantly repeated.

Give the devil his due, he had a sense of humour. Writing to his parents from prison back in 1935 when serving his first sentence of fifteen months for fraud (Mr Justice Goddard had told him that only his youth had saved him penal servitude) Haigh wrote:

> Dear Mum and Dad, ... You can't imagine me as a tailor I suppose. Well, I'm making buttonholes and trousers, waistcoats, pyjamas, pillow-slips, jackets, mail bags, coal bags, projectile bags for the navy, etc. Becoming quite accomplished in fact! but I shouldn't like to wear (outside) any of my handiwork! Mr Austin Reed would be out of business in a week—perhaps.

It is remarkable that this is the only letter in which he expresses any real remorse to his parents for the shame he had brought upon them:

> I know only too well that this is a very great and poignant greif (*sic*) and not only that a very real one to you; especially to Dad who views the subsequent dishonour to the Lord's name most seriously ... I must say now whilst I have the opportunity to express myself verbally you know I have almost always found impossible—that I am most deeply sorry for the terrible grief of which I am sensible that I have caused you: how I despise myself for the reproach and shame which I have brought upon the honour of the household. May God give me time to redeem the past and to make you happy in your latter years if this can be any recompence.

The younger Haigh ends this presumably sincere piece of soul-searching with a postscript in capital letters: PLEASE SEND ME ANOTHER PACKET OF ECLIPSE BLADES WHEN YOU WRITE.

Strange Bedfellows

For a time Prisoner No. 2074, namely John George Haigh, was in the hospital wing at Brixton. His number at Lewes was 1296 and in the condemned cell at Wandsworth he was Prisoner 7663. Prison hospital wings tend to make as strange bedfellows as the wards of hospitals on the outside. There were two other murderers there, a man named Chamberlain who had killed a woman at Exeter and a certain Cooper who had strangled his wife with a stocking at Shepherd's Bush.

Another inmate was Albert Atkinson, ten years older than Haigh and claiming that he had served with the Royal Flying Corps during the 1914–18 War. According to Gerald Byrne, he was in Brixton on a rather less serious but slightly droll charge of claiming to be 'Beachcomber' of the *Daily Express*, and thereby obtaining money by false pretences.

Atkinson described Haigh, Cooper and Chamberlain as 'three very nice fellows'. Haigh, according to Atkinson, used to taunt Cooper and Chamberlain by saying that they would hang, while he would go to Broadmoor.

According to Atkinson, Haigh said he got his idea for murder by reading a book called *Double Life* about a butcher who drank his victims' blood and sold their flesh as veal.

I have not read that edifying piece of literature, but it is probably about Fritz Haarman of Hanover who slew at least twenty-four boys and sold their flesh over the counter of his butcher's shop. Haigh may also have read about Sylvester Matuska who was charged with twenty-two murders arising from the Budapest–Ostend crash which he engineered in 1931. When the trial opened Matuska was serving six years imprisonment for train-wrecking in Austria.

'I wrecked trains because I like to see people die,' he admitted. 'I like to hear them scream. I like to see them suffer.'

Matuska was not feigning madness. In the official history of one of London's great hospitals, a nineteenth-century surgeon of high repute is said to have opposed the introduction of anaesthetics because he 'liked to hear a good healthy scream.'

It is possible that Haigh murdered for pleasure as well as profit. Haigh said he killed because he was guided by a power outside himself to do so. Matuska said, 'I acted under a hypnotic influence of a spirit named Leo.'

In the third edition of *Clinical Psychiatry*, by Mayer-Gross, Slater and Roth, (Baillière, Tindall and Cassell), twenty-one years after Haigh was hanged, it is written:

> The social and legal importance of the emotionally callous psychopath is considerable. Although extreme variants are rare, yet in greater or lesser degree, this quality of personality contributes to the make-up of society's most ruthless, dangerous and incorrigible criminals. However, it must not be assumed that the emotionally callous are invariably criminal; psychiatric experience is biased as it is only when these people are also criminal that they are likely to come under observation. There are many 'normal' men who, cold and unfeeling though they be, are also cautious, conventional and socially correct and never offend against the law. They are kept on permissible paths by prudence and considerations of expediency; and it is their subordinates, business associates, consorts and children who suffer, perhaps not through any act of spite, but through their incapacity for warmth and sympathy. Their lack of capac-

ity for human feeling, and their lack of need for the affection, the friendship and the understanding of others, is like a blind spot in the personality. Whole aspects of life mean very little to them; but that which remains may yet provide an adequate and unexceptionable field for self-expression. Some of these abnormal personalities may through sternness, ascetism and sincere ideals, win respect and regard; and they have probably played a conspicuous part in the annals of religious persecution.

Mayer-Gross, Slater and Roth have this to say about home environment:

> The child who is to grow up into a callous psychopath will have a record of another kind also. He will have been found generally unresponsive, incapable of friendship, or even of a natural affection to his parents. For reasons, into which genetical and environmental causes may both enter, his parents have frequently shown some of the same traits too, so that home life has been lacking in warmth, and the child's chances of making satisfactory adjustments have been reduced. It is remarkable how emotional callousness or coolness in one or two members of a household leads to an atmosphere of estrangement, bitterness and resentment which may spread over the life of the members of the family, destroying all warm human relations. . . .

How much of the foregoing can be applied to Haigh? And, more important, how much of it can be applied to Haigh's parents? Haigh senior's letters to brethren he was sentencing to spiritual ostracism are those of a religious bigot. If John George Haigh was a psychopath could not his father have been one, but one who kept on 'permissive paths by prudence and considerations of expediency'?

It is not suggested that Haigh's parents did not love their only child, but did their love have the warmth of natural affection, spontaneity and laughter? True, they bought him an Ark to play with, religious books at Christmas, a puppy and rabbits to keep in the back garden, but no other children were permitted into the parlour for tea or even to play Ludo, certainly not Postman's Knock.

In attempting to assess Haigh's character—and it is a formidable task—one cannot escape one very remarkable, if not unique, aspect of him. As a child, an angelic, sweet-natured child according to his Mum and Dad, he had no friends. Yet as an adult, when he had departed from the paths of righteousness, became an unscrupulous rogue and ultimately a mass murderer, a calculating murderer, he had plenty of friends. Moreover, his friends were not villains. They varied from nice young girls to nice old ladies, from concert pianists to respectable painters. He moved in polite circles, not thieves' kitchens.

It is true that Haigh's letters to his parents do not suggest an embittered home with an atmosphere of estrangement. His letters are gaily bantering—'To the dearest old dad in the world'—he says in one, but Dr Noël C. Browne has pointed out that the written word is often more suspect that the spoken one.

The girl Haigh constantly refers to in his letters is Ba—Barbara Stephens; and if Haigh was capable of being in love, *if* I say, then he was in love with Barbara Stephens. She certainly deserved the love of a better man. She was only fifteen when they first met, much younger than Haigh. For a while he lived in her parents' house at Crawley as one of the family.

Barbara Stephens was Haigh's constant escort at concerts. Music was their mutual passion. One can imagine with what horror this young girl must have read the sickening details of the crimes committed by her charming companion, a man so much older than herself, but so platonically devoted to her.

She emerges from the ordeal with credit. She visited him frequently when he was in prison at Lewes and Brixton awaiting trial and moved from her Crawley home to the old Star and Garter Hotel, Brighton, whilst the trial was in progress.

Lewes couldn't accommodate the army of reporters covering the sensational Haigh case and the overflow stayed at the Star and Garter, for many years a rendezvous for newspapermen. Consequently, Barbara was quizzed by them unmercifully in the hope that she might reveal something salacious, but she did nothing of the kind.

She said nothing to discredit Haigh, declined to have anything to do with the cheque-book journalism rampant among Sunday newspapers, refused large sums of money to talk about her friendship with him.

Two days after Haigh had been sentenced to death, this brave and steadfast girl wrote to his aged parents:

> Dear Mr and Mrs Haigh,
>
> I'm afraid there's nothing much I can say that will be of any avail because I know exactly the way you must be feeling. I am completely heartbroken about the whole affair and at the moment I feel as though I am living in a dream.
>
> I have been staying at the above hotel during the trial, because it's nearer than Crawley. I saw John after the verdict for about three minutes and you will be glad to know that he was completely calm and composed.
>
> Please accept my deepest sympathies and I only wish there was something I could do and say that would help you.
>
> With very kindest regards,
> Yours sincerely,
> Barbara Stephens.

One cannot help wondering how a man so coldly callous, so sly and pitiless a murderer as John George Haigh could have inspired such devotion in the breast of a transparently good and intelligent girl. It is easy to picture him ingratiating himself with the old ladies who sat around—and still do—the Onslow Court Hotel.

'They positively fluttered when he paused to chat them up,' the head porter of that most respectable establishment, told me. 'Then, of course, remember rationing still existed and Haigh could get them almost any little luxuries that was in short supply—at a price, of course.'

Mrs Durand-Deacon paid the highest price.

One the 26th of July, 1949, Barbara Stephens was back home

at Crawley. On the Sunday previously, Haigh had celebrated his fortieth birthday, if celebrated is the right verb.

Dear Mr and Mrs Haigh, (Barbara Stephens wrote. Thank you for your letters and I realise how difficult it must be for you to write. Please don't bother to acknowledge this note.

I didn't do anything about John's birthday, it was so awkward being on a Sunday for one thing and it was so difficult to know what to say in the circumstances. I don't know whether you have received any communication from him but he hasn't written to me.

When I saw him I asked whether he wanted to see me again and he said no, he thought it would be better for both of us if I didn't visit him again. I believe it would be possible for him to have visitors if he desired it. Much as I should love to see him, I shall abide by what he says.

I'm afraid there's absolutely nothing I can say which will lessen your grief in any way, as I know only too well.

With all my love to you both,

Yours very sincerely,

Barbara.

John George Haigh had, in fact, written to his parents from the death cell at Wandsworth on his fortieth birthday, Sunday, July 24th:·

Dearest Mum & Dad:

I believe I have already acknowledged your xx. Thanks also for your xxl with cutting. A very good photograph. . . .

Thank you also for the very beautiful card recd. yesterday. They are really beautiful flowers and what a delightful little dresden figure too. It's a wonderful day although the heat is terrific. I don't remember such a succession of torrid week ends for years. I am sure that if I was outside and had arranged to go to the coast or somewhere it would be raining. True: Ba can see me although I told her some time that I wouldn't do so after the trial (in here). I did see her for a few minutes before leaving

Lewes. We shall not appeal as there was nothing in the summing up to which exception can be taken. I've no doubt he intended it to be a classic and it certainly was. He could not be accused of misdirection. I shall rely purely upon consideration of the case by the Home Office. It's a pity I'm not allowed newspapers as I'm sure today's must be interesting. Eager* came to see me yesterday and I have arranged for him to organise your journey with Sommerfield† should you desire to make it. He will of course see that all your comforts are provided for. But of course if you prefer the company of someone like Geo. Grant you could come down with him and leave Sommerfield to organise your accommodation at this end. Again I remind you that visiting conditions will not be all that you would desire: there will not be the same open facilities as would have been available at Lewes or even Brixton.

I have had a letter from Sophie which is really a masterpiece in noncommittance. It was clearly patent that it was not an easy letter to write. She said that should you come to London she would much regret not seeing you. You know her 'phone number but in case it is misplaced it is Freemantle 2622.

I shall put up my improvised sunblind and retire from the tropical heat so far as it can be evaded. Leaving you to the design of an almighty spirit whose motif is written and is inscrutable. All my love, Sonnie.

On the 20th of the month he had written to his parents:

You will have heard the verdict and by now you will have read about yesterday's proceedings in the paper. . . . Ba was there and was of course upset . . . but she nevertheless took the judgment very bravely. Remember that there is still a Daniel's God today and that the Great Spirit of Infinity is not impotent and therefore this is no final judgment as yet. Though all things are already written whatever they be. The position so

* Mr Ireland Eager, Haigh's solicitor.

† Mr Stafford Sommerfield, a *News of the World* feature writer, afterwards Editor.

far is quite as we expected it to be. I am now at Wandsworth... which is rather grim, but 3 people* living together in silence as I have no desire for protracted conversation below my intellectual level.... Fondest love—Sonnie

On the first of August the pianist Albert Ferber once again writes to him, this time wishing he could play to him at Wandsworth. He wrote from Cholmely Gardens, NW6:

My dear John,

I can't remember whether I had ever written to you that I have had a letter from the Chaplain at Brixton, a very nice one, thanking me for the offer but he said that as they had only short time prisoners they had no facilities.

What about the present? Do please let me know if there is anything at all that I can do. I wish I could come and see you. Can I? What is your position now? Is one allowed to send you things? Have you all you want? Please drop me a line if you can think of anything you might like.

I still wish I could come and play to you. I know they've got a piano in the hall because I remember playing Chopin on it one Sunday afternoon. But perhaps you are not allowed to go there? I have no idea of the regulations. But I would gladly pay for the transport up the stairs.

Will you let me know whether you receive this note? I hope you do if only to let you know I have not forgotten you or ever will.

With all my very best thoughts,

Albert Ferber.

Albert Ferber did, in fact, go to see Haigh in the condemned cell. The man who was so soon to die told his parents 'Of course, he couldn't bring a piano on a barrow like the man at Outwood.'

A macabre joke, perhaps, but in villages like Outwood, near

* Haigh is referring to the two prison officers who were always in attendance with a condemned, known as 'death watch screws'.

Wakefield, people did have furniture moved—and removed—by barrow.

The dreadful thing, of course, is that a few days later Haigh's own body was being pushed on a trolley from the execution pit at Wandsworth to the mortuary, where on one occasion, according to Molly Lefeburg, the hangman put his head inside the door and asked Dr Keith Simpson who was about to carry out a post-mortem, 'Can I have a look at my handiwork, sir?'

It is quite likely that Haigh, like Petiot, who was guillotined in 1946 for murdering twenty-seven people in a gas chamber of his own design in his house in the Rue Lebseur, Paris, murdered for pleasure as well as profit.

This is a frightful thing, but is it any more horrifying than the fact that before judicial murder was abolished in this country the Home Office used to receive a minimum of fifty unsolicited applications a year for the post of official hangman? Were these applications from law-abiding citizens prompted entirely by a sense of social conscience? Should not the would-be executioners be subjected to psychiatric treatment to the same degree as murderers?

Psychiatry is still in its infancy. The axioms of a few years ago are now regarded as shibboleths. The pronouncements of some of the leading savants in this important, but by no means exact, medical science, are manifestly absurd. They are as vulnerable as the rest of us, so what hopes has a jury of workaday men and women got of arriving at a rightful conclusion regarding any man's sanity?

Take the great Dr Jung, of Zurich, one of the most famous psychoanalysts. He read the entire 735 pages of James Joyce's *Ulysses* and came to the conclusion that nothing of any importance happened on 'Bloomsday', Thursday, June 16th, 1904.

Frank Budgen, in his *James Joyce and The Making of Ulysses*, has this pertinent comment to make on the learned doctor's findings:

> It is always difficult to agree with anybody about what is important, yet if we enumerate the things that happen in

Ulysses most human beings will agree of themselves apart from the manner of presentation, these happenings are important. Included in them are a funeral, a fight, political discord, an act of seduction, one of adultery, the birth of a child, a drunken orgy, a rupture of friendship and the loss of a position. A new theory as to the character and dominant motive of the great poet (Shakespeare) is expounded. Domestic beasts, on which the life of human society largely depends, are smitten with a dread disease and the community brings its varied intelligence to bear on a means to end that plague. Acts of charity, both public and private, are performed and acts of treachery as well. True, there is no declaration of war with proclamations and the calling out of fighting men, no revolutions with conspirators issuing from cellars to take command of the state, but war and revolution are present in the memories and aspirations of the characters of the book. The Boer War and the Russo-Japanese War are living memories and the Sinn Fein Party is actively organizing the citizens of Ireland for rupture with Great Britain and the setting up of a separate state.

And the great Dr Jung finds nothing of importance in all this turmoil and turpitude so vividly described by Joyce! Perhaps Dr Jung did not understand it. How then did it come about that he founded a school of psychoanalysis? If I digress, I do so deliberately. Dr Jung's offhand opinion reminds me of Dr Yellowlees' dictum in regard to Haigh's letters; 'Burn them!'

If prison and hospitals make strange bedfellows, so often do society marriages. One has only to spend a day in a divorce court to discover that, and the seamier newspapers have never ceased to regret the day when the Act was passed forbidding the reporting of evidence given in this type of case.

John George Haigh and his wife never got around to a divorce. For those who believe that one's destiny is influenced by the signs of the Zodiac, it might be interesting to reflect that Haigh was born under the sign of Leo, July 24th, 1909, and was hanged under the sign of the same constellation, August 6th,

1949. He was married at Bridlington, Yorkshire, on July 6th, 1934.

His bride was Beatrice Hamer, known as Betty. Their family backgrounds could scarcely have been in greater contrast. Haigh's parents were intensely, almost dementedly religious. Betty Hamer's father and mother were 'on the halls.'

Despite having once done a stint as what is called a 'show biz reporter', I could not remember any music hall act named Hamer. However, the truly encyclopaedic memory of 'Wee Georgie Wood' came to my help. George, himself a great star of the good old days of the music hall, remembered the act well. Betty's father was Harold Clisby Hamer, from Stockport.

'When Arthur Godfrey was divorced by his wife, Minnie Duncan, the act of Duncan and Godfrey was reformed as *The Coster's Wedding,*' George told me. 'It started with the song,

Today's the Day the Wedding Bells will Ring,
Today's the Day I'll Do the Proper Fing,
Though yer Name's Brown Now,
Just 'Old Yer Row
I'm Going Ter Change it Soon,
The Parson's There what's Going to Marry Us,
A Donkey Cart is Going to Carry Us,
And When the Knot is Tied
And You're the Blushing Bride,
We're a goin' on our Honeymoon.

'Minnie Duncan—or Madame Godfrey as she insisted on being called then teamed up 'Happy' Hamer. Their act was also a cockney and they opened up with,

I've lost my heart
To Napoleon Bonaparte,
I would have been
A far better Queen
Than Marie Louise or Josephine,
I'd Have helped Him to Win at Waterloo,

When He Crossed the Alps I'd 'Ave Crossed them Too,
St Helena,
He'd Have Never Been There
Had I been Missus Napoleon.

George recalled that he was on the same bill with 'Happy' Hamer and Madame Godfrey at Leeds Hippodrome round about 1912. When he returned from America in 1916, the act had become Hamer and Hamer. Again George was on the same bill with them and the opening had been changed to 'Happy' Hamer, dressed as an urchin, singing,

I have lost my daddy,
My daddy's far away,
He's Up in Heaven They Say,
Oh—O—O, Daddy was a Bookie
Who Never Could Bet Square
They're Laying Six to Four
They Know Where he's Gone
But My Mum Lays Odds on He Isn't There.

'Incidentally,' says George. 'Although Earl Wilson and others attribute to Milton Berle the title of "The Thief of Bad Gags" it was actually given to "Happy" Hamer by Malcolm Scott, the music hall's greatest wit—whose act as Katherine Parr the "Last Wife of Henry the Vee and Three Eyes" was a classic of music hall comedy.'

The digression is not so inconsequential as it might seem. The family backgrounds of bride and groom could scarcely have differed more widely. The idea of 'Happy' Hamer's daughter marrying the son of two religious bigots like the Haighs is incongruous, to say the least. By comparison, a marriage between a Montagu and a Capulet would have been plain sailing. Not surprisingly, the ceremony at Bridlington Registry Office was not graced by the presence of any of the parents-in-law.

Both bride and groom gave their address as the Alexandra Hotel, Bridlington. It is possible that Betty Hamer thought that

Haigh was a wealthy young man about that little seaside town. He was driving an Alfa Romeo car. She was soon disillusioned. In November of the same year Haigh was arrested on the charge of conspiring to defraud, aiding and abetting the forgery of a document and obtaining money by false pretences. The probability is that Haigh did not aid and abet the forgery as much as commit it himself, but at that time his dubious talent was not known to the police.

Haigh was in prison when a daughter was born to Betty. He never claimed paternity and there is no record that Betty ever visited him in prison. She did stay for a while with Haigh's parents, but it was a stay of very short duration. Eventually, Betty had the baby, Pauline, adopted. Haigh never saw the child. In fact, he only saw his wife on one occasion after his release.

It was a chance encounter in the street, Haigh no longer owning an Alfa Romeo. He told his wife, 'I think you ought to know that we're not really married. I have another wife living. I married her before I met you.'

Betty Haigh, *née* Hamer, was perhaps more relieved than heart-broken. She joined the WAAF at the outbreak of the 1939–45 War and became a sergeant, employed on radar, guiding night fighters. She later married an RAF navigator named Adam Stewart. He was shot down over the Bay of Biscay in June, 1943. In September of the same year she married Denis Alan Neale, at Sandwich, Kent.

After the war they went to live in a picturesque cottage at Rock, near Bodmin, Cornwall. She called herself Wendy Neale.

Ten days after Haigh was executed they went through another ceremony at Bodmin Register Office to confirm their marital status.

The best man at the Bodmin ceremony was the late Mr Duncan Webb, a *Sunday People* reporter. As the ceremony was held on Saturday morning it was well-timed for that newspaper to obtain a scoop, but aggravating for the *News of the World*, the paper that had paid for Haigh's defence.

'Tommie' Duncan Webb subsequently married Mrs Donald

Hume, previously the wife of the murderer of Setty whose dismembered torso he dropped from an aircraft into the sea, near Southend. Hume was found guilty of the murder to which he subsequently confessed after serving ten years on the lesser charge of disposing of the body, being set free to murder on at least two more occasions and is now serving life imprisonment in Switzerland. As soon as Hume's wife got her divorce she married Duncan Webb, which tends to indicate that crime-reporting can also lead to strange bedfellowship.

The Age of the Pin-Table Machine

In December, 1935, Haigh was released from his first prison sentence. In a moment of uncharacteristic remorse, he had written to Mum and Dad: 'May God give me time to redeem the past and to make you happy in your latter years.' Perhaps he meant it. He did indeed return to the parental roof for a while, 'Grange View', Ledger Lane, Outwood. Having done time for fraudulent hire-purchase deals, selling non-existent motor cars, he decided to go into the dry-cleaning business. 'You can't go wrong,' he said, but he could and did. He decided that it would be more profitable to take people to the cleaners. Leeds wasn't big enough to hold John George Haigh or his ambitions.

One can imagine his grey-haired mother waving him goodbye as he set off for London. It was the age of pin-table machines. One-armed bandits were still illegal and were only to be found in the sleazier afternoon clubs, always liable to be raided by squads of police in vans. Pin-table machines of the type which would now be considered somewhat unsophisticated escaped the vigilance of the Law because it was deemed that an element of skill was involved in their manipulation.

Almost every public house had a pin-table machine and every High Street an arcade full of them. Today they would be considered museum pieces of the funfair world, although they still remain a craze in French cafés.

Among the many people who made fortunes out of the pin-table craze in England during the thirties was a Mr McSwan, of Woodside, Wimbledon. For more than ten years Mr McSwan and his son, Donald, had been members of the Amusement Caterers' Association of which Sir Billy Butlin was at one time president.

Out of the profits from the pin-table machines the McSwans had acquired property at Raynes Park and Beckenham. Mr McSwan decided that he needed a chauffeur/secretary, an odd combination of jobs and he advertised the vacancy in that old-established journal of funfair and circus folk, *World's Fair.*

Your guess is as good as mine as to what prompted John George Haigh to buy a copy, but he did. He applied for the job by telegram and got it. Mr McSwan was 'well pleased' with his new employee and Haigh was soon promoted to be manager of a saloon at Tooting.

Within nine years, Mr and Mrs McSwan and their son, Donald, had all been liquidated—literally. The strange thing is that the disappearance of the family went unreported and nobody suspected foul play until Haigh confessed to murdering them.

They were all alive and well when Haigh left their employment to start up in business on his own.

He set up in business as a solicitor, adopting a name he had taken from the Law List. He would then advertise that he was winding up an estate and had shares to dispose of at below market prices. From would-be investors he asked a mere 25 per cent deposit. The cheques rolled in. As soon as they were cleared he would move to another district to continue his swindling, again using the name of a genuine solicitor.

Spelling was not his great forte and he came unstuck when he started operations at Guildford. On his letter heading, he left the *d* out of the name of that Surrey town. It is surprising that the printer didn't notice the error, but when a solicitor can't spell the name of the town in which he has an office even the most gullible of prospective investors in likely to start making inquiries before reaching for his cheque book. This slip on Haigh's part hardly qualifies him as 'perhaps the most accomplished criminal of the century.'

It cost Haigh four years penal servitude at Surrey Assizes, Kingston, on November 24th, 1937. When he came out of gaol the second World War was hotting up. Haigh became a fire-watcher.

From his lodgings at 26 James Street, London, W1, he writes to his parents on November 17th, 1940:

Dear Mum and Dad,

I think I'll start this while I've still got pen & ink & gas and a table left to write it on.

Last night was certainly the worst we have had around here. We must have been doing some damage in Berlin. I went to bed as usual and went soundly to sleep at 8.30. The drone of a plane or two above not being of much consequence these days. It was also raining which made a peaceful night seem almost certain. It stopped raining however later on and then the fun began. What a birthday! I'm telling you that you can't imagine what is was like. I was awakened about 11.30 by quite a heavy barage (*sic*). Then I dozed off again, because at 2.10 a.m. precisely I was awakened by a most terrific thunderclap. That was No. 1 which dropped near the corner of Selfridge's in Oxford Street. I got up, opened the window and had a look out but couldn't see anything. But about 10 minutes later the glare from a fire which the explosion had started at a gas main lit up my room. My bed is alongside the window so I sat up to watch. It was now 2.25 and I heard the familiar swish coming. It seemed as though it went passed (*sic*) my window but of course it would be sixty ft. above. I ducked my head under the pillow, because the least I expected was the windows coming in. There was the most unholy crash followed by the jingle of falling glass then silence. So removed myself from the underside of the pillow, ostrichwise, and took another look out and said 'That's a close one that was' (with apologies to Shell) I couldn't see anything for a few minutes on account of the dust, but when it cleared I found that the C. & A. store opposite was badly blown about. The bomb dropped inside and blew two walls out. There is a big public shelter underneath and fortunately no one was hurt, although they had to evacuate. Following that bombs continued to fall for the best part of two hours and during that time I counted fifty-two that were within earshot. I might tell you the house didn't shake. It rocked. I myself and the bloke next door decided it was a little late to start going over to Wigmore Street and we stayed put. It was quite a rough passage but we are still alive to tell the tale so why worry? They plastered the West End badly as a whole I found this morning. Among the places hit was the National Gallery (Trafalgar Square) the Strand Palace, the Savoy & Covent Garden Station, Hamptons (furnishers) is still ablaze—that is, it was about 2.30 p.m. They made a mess of Waterloo station also.

Poor old Coventry got an awful wallopping, didn't it? After reading of it I was very glad to receive your letter indicating that 43 Stainburn Drive* still existed. I was anxious until it arrived although not desparately (*sic*) so because I felt that had anything happened Winifred would have let me know straight away.

Bless her little heart; tell her that I don't flirt with Mona. Mona flirts with me, by the look of things. Thank her for her note please and say that I am pleased her accident didn't totally disable her caligraphic (*sic*) ability. Tell her that I've got a bit of a dash on Clara; she's a much nicer girl than Mona. . . .

Yours affectionately, Sonnie.

Lonely schoolboy he might have been, but Haigh did not lack girl friends as a young man. They wrote to him even when he went to prison, although they came from respectable working class homes, some as religious as his own.

'You know the saying, dear, "it is never too late to mend" ', one writes to him. 'I am going to put all my trust in our Dear Lord and I know he will help me to do what is right.

* The Haighs had moved to Leeds.

'My Dear one, you ought to be coming for your dinner, I am making it today, my mother has gone to church and left me to do the cooking. So if you see any Deaths in the paper you will know where it is. Mother says practise makes perfect.

'John Darling, Don't you start having headaches, it is only me that should have them but I shall be alright by the time you come home. I have never been so ill as I was on Friday. I don't know what was the matter with me & of course everybody said it was you had left me and to finish up I had to work until late, my mother was vexed with me for staying but I am alright now, and I hope you are too....

'Just finished dinner so now I must finish your letter, because I would like to post it & then you can get it in the morning, won't you sweet one. I may be going to Horsforth next week-end. I ought to have gone today but I had this letter to write....

'Do you know sweetheart where I am writing this letter—in the bathroom now don't laugh.

'I was wondering this morning what Roundhay and Kirkstall is looking like it is such a long time since we were there.... I am going to church tonight and I will ask our Dear Lord to send you safely back home to me and if it is his wish to make us both one. John I need you, but I need our Dear Lord more, he comes first and I hope He always will, and also I pray that your Mother & Father will love me too for your sake because I always shall as if they were my own.

'Darling I shall have to close it is nearly for the post and I don't want to miss it so I will write again soon, so with my little snap I close but I shall always remain yours for ever and ever.

Goodbye for the present, Darling,

Bobbie xxxxxxxx

In June 1941 he was sentenced at London Sessions to twenty-one months hard labour for stealing five bunks and kitchen material worth £17 10s and also stealing, while acting as bailee, sixty yards of curtaining and a refrigerator.

Yet he evinced a disdain for the average criminal, calling most of them 'cheap crooks'. It is alleged that in Lincoln Prison he told fellow inmates, 'If you're going crooked, do it in a big way—go after rich old women who like a bit of flattery.'

Haigh was employed in the tinsmith's shop at Lincoln where sulphuric acid was in use and accessible. Other prisoners who worked outside captured field mice for him and he experimented with the rodents in jars of concentrated acid.

In 1944, he went to live at Northgate Road, Crawley, with the parents of Barbara Stephens. At the time she was still a schoolgirl. He writes:

> Dearest Mum & Dad, I don't know why we all felt tired: it must be the weather. Of course, Barbara and I could account for it by a late night we had on Thursday. She came up to town from school and we went to see Everyman, Les Syphildes and Spanish Dances by the International Ballet. It was marvellous you'd have enjoyed the Spanish Dances. They had wonderful long dresses with high shoes and mantillas and they accompanied their dances with castagnettes (*sic*). Ba was very thrilled with it. She looked very lovely that night. She wore a grey flannel costume with a light green jumper which she had knit herself. It looks terribly smart. We got back home at 10 to 11.
>
> I know you read between the lines too easily. I suppose it is a very close friendship we have formed and I am very fond of her in a brotherly sort of fashion. Whether anything else will develop from it at a date I don't know. Remember she is only 16½. At this moment I am quite content that we find each others company so pleasing. It has its drawbacks of course. It means that when our company is so mutually necessary that we find it a little unbearable when we are alone. Ba said to me . . . that Mon-Thurs was intolerably long & Thurs-Mon always flew so desperately quickly. She's a little kid who if ever you meet her am sure you would like . . .

In the same year Haigh met Donald McSwan again in the *Goat* public house, Kensington. Over the beers young McSwan told

Haigh he was a bit concerned about the call-up. No patriot he.

Haigh advised him to 'go on the trot', to get lost or run away. If he wasn't at home, he couldn't receive calling-up papers, could he? Donald McSwan saw the logic of this, but where would he go? It wasn't so easy, what with ration cards and things.

Haigh told him not to worry. Anyway, this was neither the time nor the place for such a discussion. Haigh himself had evaded the call-up. He knew the ropes. It was a question of 'follow me, McSwan'.

McSwan did. He would have been better advised to wait for his call-up papers.

The two young men met frequently. The McSwans were living in Claverton Street, Pimlico, and Donald's parents gave a big welcome to the erstwhile manager of their Tooting saloon.

They were not actively concerned with the pin-table business quite so much now, what with the doodle-bombs and the blitz and glass being so hard to come by. They were more or less retired. What was Haigh up to?

Well, Haigh had taken a leaf out of their book, in a manner of speaking. He'd set up on his own, repairing pin-table machines.

To that end he'd found a basement in Gloucester Road, 79 to be precise. The rent was only £7 a month. He lived nearby at Queen's Gate, bed-sitter land.

The McSwans reckoned Haigh was on to a good thing. Haigh told Donald he must come round to his workshop some time. Donald did several times, once too often.

It was on September 9th, 1944, that John George Haigh lifted a pin-table leg and battered Donald McSwan to death in the basement at 79 Gloucester Road.

Haigh alleged that he made an incision in the victim's neck. 'I got a mug and took some blood from his neck and drank it. Then I realised I must do something about him. I left him there dead.

'I had acid and sheet metal for pickling. I found a water butt on a disused site and took it on a cart and put McSwan in acid. I put the body in the tub and poured acid in with a bucket.'

Then Haigh went round to see McSwan's parents, telling them that Donald had 'gone on the trot' to avoid the call-up. He was quite safe, the military would never catch up with him now. So the parents were not in the least surprised when they received a letter in what looked like their son's hand-writing and date-stamped Glasgow. It wasn't their son's writing. It was a forgery by Haigh. There was no address on the letter, which was natural enough, their boy being of no fixed abode now, but well looked after.

It had taken Haigh seventy-four hours to dispose of Donald McSwan's remains. The acid solution wasn't working quickly enough for his liking, so he went to Gamages and bought a large mincer and a cleaver. He greased the floor of the cellar before cutting up the body so that no blood stains would be left.

Conveniently for Haigh, there was a drain in the basement, down which he poured the last of Donald McSwan. Mr and Mrs McSwan continued to receive letters purporting to come from their son, asking them to send him money, *via* John George Haigh as he was the only chap he could trust, the only friend who knew his whereabouts. The truth of this was ironic.

Then Haigh became impatient over the small sums of money he was getting out of the McSwans—or they got suspicious. So he lured them round to the basement in Gloucester Road on the pretext of meeting Donald who was in London for a few hours.

Haigh might well have said 'Mind your head!' as the old folk entered the dark cellar. He battered them to death and their remains went down the drain.

It was now time for Haigh to bring Donald McSwan back to life. He did this by posing as young McSwan himself, forging his signature on a power of attorney. This document gave Haigh four freehold properties, 9 Grand Drive, Raynes Park; 104 Kenilworth Avenue, Wimbledon Park, 15 Wimborne Way, Beckenham and 112 Churchfields Road in the same area.

He also forged transfers for £2,107 worth of gilt-edged securities held by the McSwans. Altogether, he netted about £4,000—and for that he admitted to killing three people. He had already moved into the Onslow Court Hotel, then as now a most respectable establishment catering for oldish ladies and gentlemen. He was an immediate favourite with some of the old ladies but annoyed some of the old gentlemen there by 'monopolising the telephone'. Quite a number of the calls were to bookmakers and the money for which he had murdered dwindled rapidly.

By August, 1947, Haigh was £25 5s 2d in the red.

On the other side of the Park, at Notting Hill Gate, lived a Dr and Mrs Henderson. Archie Henderson had studied medicine at Edinburgh. He was tall, good-looking and well-tailored, invariably wearing a carnation in his lapel and a clipped moustache on his upper lip, as became an officer who had served in the Royal Army Medical Corps.

His Chelsea marriage in 1930 to Frances Dorothy Orr was one of the events of the season. She was the daughter of a Glasgow solicitor, but unfortunately she died suddenly while the couple were staying with her husband at Bailey's Hotel in the Gloucester Road. An inquest was held and Bernard Spilsbury testified that Mrs Henderson, who was thirty-six, had died from 'natural causes'. She left a substantial fortune and for a time, at any rate, Dr Henderson wasn't entirely dependent upon medicine.

The Hendersons had become friendly with a Mr and Mrs Erren. Rudolf Erren was a German and had flown with Richtofen's Circus in the 1914–18 War. Rose, his wife, was a Manchester girl, quite remarkably attractive. Her photograph had been published in beauty competitions.

In 1938 Erren was interned and eventually sent to Canada on the ill-fated *Arandora Star*. He was one of the few survivors.

His marriage however did not survive, however, for Rose Erren had an affair with the widowed Archie Henderson. Erren named Henderson in his divorce suit and went back to the Fatherland. Rose married Archie.

Archie Henderson had bought a practice at Upminster and was also medical officer to the Essex County Constabulary. Upminster palled on them after ten months and they looked for somewhere nearer the West End. Both Archie and Rose were night-club types. He gambled heavily and drank a bottle of whisky a day.

Eventually they found a place at 22 Ladbroke Square, W11 but they must have been living it up beyond the income from Archie's practice because Rose used the upper rooms as a guest house. Even this additional income proved inadequate and they advertised the house for sale.

Among those who called in response to the advertisement was John George Haigh, who agreed to take the place for more than the asking price.

'Of the scores of stupid people I've met, I've just been introduced to the greatest of them all,' Rose Henderson wrote to her brother in Manchester. 'I offered him 22 Ladbroke Square, lock, stock and barrel for £7,750, and he said "That's too cheap, but if you will accept ten thousand, it's a deal." '

Rose Henderson's brother wrote back to her, 'When you meet a man like that you should run for your life.'

It is a pity that Rose didn't take her brother's advice. Haigh never did buy 22 Ladbroke Square. He always had a glib excuse about money being tied up and waiting for his trustee to release some shares.

So eventually the Hendersons, tiring of Haigh's excuses, sold the house to a genuine customer, and bought 16 Dawes Road, Fulham, the ground floor being a Doll's Hospital and flats over the shop. The astonishing thing is that Haigh remained friends with the Hendersons, despite having failed to complete the deal.

'I found them interesting and amusing,' Haigh wrote. 'And we went around a good deal together. They used to like me to play to them and for many hours I sat at their piano interpreting the classics.'

Moving as they did in the pseudo-*blasé* atmosphere of the night-club circuit one would have thought that the Hendersons would have seen through a *shyster* like Haigh. They had both been around. They were not starry-eyed, like Barbara Stephens, that brave and steadfast little heroine. Their world was slightly more sophisticated than that of the pin-table arcade. And Archie was a doctor.

'Studying the Haigh case,' Dr Noël C. Browne said to me, 'I feel that his victims were as much in need of psychiatric treatment as Haigh himself.'

The scene moves to the Metropole Hotel, Brighton. The Hendersons are staying there with their red setter, Pat.

John George Haigh is now £237 and 10d overdrawn at the Westminster Bank, Gloucester Road. He also owed £400 to a money-lender as well as his bill at the Onslow Court.

'During this period my dream cycle had commenced,' Haigh confessed.

He was seized with the urge to drink blood. 'I saw a forest of crucifixes which changed to trees dripping blood; once more I wakened with the desire which demanded fulfilment.

'Archie was to be the next victim. I drove him to Crawley and in the store room at Leopold Road I shot him in the head with his own revolver, which I had taken from Dawes Road.

'I then returned to Brighton, and told Rose that Archie had been taken ill very suddenly and needed her. I said I would drive her to him. She accompanied me to the store room at Crawley and there I shot her. From each of them I took my draught of blood.'

Well, that was Haigh's story and he was going to stick to it. In his diary for that date, February 12th, 1948, the sign of the cross was written in red crayon and the initials *A.H.* and *R.H.* There was a similar entry for September 9th, 1944, the date on which he killed Donald McSwan. This, too, was marked with a cross.

On February 16th, 1948, the day following the murder of the Hendersons, Haigh arrived at the Metropole and paid their bill, producing what appeared to be a letter of authority signed by Archie Henderson. He took the red setter for a walk on the beach and then had the Hendersons possessions and luggage loaded onto his car, including two golf bags.

On the previous day he had paid £505 into his account and this was followed by another cheque for £200 from Horace Sidney Bull, a Horsham jeweller.

On March 11th his account was credited with another £10—this from Mrs Durand-Deacon. He had sold her Mrs Henderson's handbag.

It's a wonder he didn't sell the red setter, but he placed it in kennels.

He got £400 for Archie Henderson's car and with forged deeds obtained possession of 16 Dawes Road, Fulham. That year Haigh paid over £7,700 into his account. It is difficult to get away from Professor Keith Simpson's terse description of him as 'a shrewd, tough little business man'.

He had acquired a Lagonda car but in June, 1948, it was found at the foot of Beachy Head, having crashed over the cliff. The unidentified body of a woman was found nearby. That mystery has never been solved and although he confessed to nine murders Haigh strenuously denied being involved in the tragedy.

If, as has been alleged, Haigh admitted to more murders than he actually committed in order to get himself a ticket to Broadmoor, why did he not admit to this one?

The New Year finds him in right good spirits and staying at the George Hotel, Crawley. Never was there a murderer who wrote to many cheerful Mum and Dad letters, full of inconsequential chitchat.

On January 1st, 1949 he writes:

Dearest Mum and Dad,

Hope you received my New Year Telegram. I rather fancy you did because it might have given you the inspiration to send Barbara hers. It was a very good idea: she was quite pleased with it and I thought it was very well worded.

I expect you will be hanging on to the postman's tails awaiting a budget of the Christmas holiday so budget I suppose it will have to be.

I did have a very wonderful Christmas really although it was a little difficult getting a foot into everybodies camp. You would forgive my not writing over the Christmas week end I am sure it's not easy to disassociate oneself from a party of people—especially when its freezing at anything more than 2 yard from the fire!

I started quite early—on Tuesday 21st as a matter of fact. There was a party organised by a man who is in the film business and who stays at the hotel. We went first of all to a private film studio at Clapham to see a film and then about 9.30 to the Savoy for dinner which we left at about 1.30 a.m. It was all very good and I thoroughly enjoyed it. Most of the people were from the Hotel including the Manageress and the Secretary; but the new ones were quite interesting. One man in particular being quite amusing and one of the women was very charming. It may have been her dress which was attractive but I think she had some personal charm as well. There is doubt of course that everyone looks his or her best in evening dress. On the Thursday I went over to Hazel's to collect my cake. But first I got caught up with the Stone's (Managing Director of Callenders Cables) after dinner and along with Diana and a certain Swarbrick went up to their room to get 'wrapped up with a little Ancient Tapestry' (the latter being a brand of whisky).

From there we go to Midnight Mass at All Saints, Margaret Street. They sang Gounod which gave the boys voices an excellent chance to shew themselves. Then home to bye-byes. Ba went back on Christmas Day. (She wishes now she hadn't).

Tom, Trish and Rose came over to me for dinner. The girls looked absolutely devastating in the dresses and were the comment of the Hotel. Rose was in a purple and goes off the shoulder job. Trish had a pearly grey dress over which she wore a black lace Spanish shawl. She looked very fetching.

One wonders whether, as he writes, he spares a thought for the other Rose.

He records the fact that he has received 26 cards and thanks his parents for the tie—'it's heavenly'.

Before another New Year dawns the tie will be adorning

Haigh's effigy in Madame Tussaud's, together with the Lovat suit of which he is so proud.

He will be forty this year and needs glasses for reading. He wears Archie Henderson's gold-rimmed ones.

Haigh and Princess Margaret, and his Last Letter

If Haigh had a pin-up girl it was Princess Margaret. In speech and in correspondence, he goes on and on about her. Awaiting trial for his life, he does not appear to be concerned about his own neck, but gets all hot under the collar because Princess Margaret has been the subject of criticism.

I think the 'Wee Frees'* who felt it their duty to deplore her visit to the Vatican were going too far, [He writes to Mum and Dad]. I understand that the Free Church would deprecate official contact with Rome; but I don't see how any reasonable person can criticise her for making a purely personal courtesy visit to the Pope. Nobody I imagine would blame a Roman Catholic princess, if, visiting this country from abroad, should she call on the Archbishop of Canterbury, or even took tea with the Moderator of the Assembly of the Kirk of Scotland. Very well, then; surely the Wees Frees might use a little common sense to appreciate that Princess Margaret did neither more nor less than was expected of her when she paid her ceremonial and diplomatic respects to one of the most influential personages in the world.

Her deportment certainly provoked most praiseworthy comment from that person and was a very honourable reflection on

* Members of the Free Church of Scotland.

our Royal family. In these days when we are represented abroad by uncouth colliers and railway clerks, I should think the visit was worth its weight in gold. What was to be deplored—as usual—the press. They showed no discretion whatever.

In a later letter from prison, he is delighted that Princess Margaret has been made Cover Girl of the American *Time*:

Very good, I thought. Especially the bit about 'do you know you are looking into the most beautiful eyes in England?' I reckon she's a bit of a card altogether. But they are both ideal Princesses. Nigel Moneo used to tell about them when he went to paint the corgis. They are apparently quite a pair to cope with offstage.

Again, he writes:

I am going to send you a copy of the *People* which I don't suppose you get. It contains a remarkably good article about Princess Margaret. A beautiful photograph of her in Italy. If the press had confined themselves such photographs of her holiday there would have been some sense in it. Some of the anecdotes recounted therein are very amusing just like what Nigel told us after he'd been to Buck House painting the dogs. I love the one about the shaving. And the bit about 'Not before the Minister, Margaret' made me hoot with laughter you'll probably think it funny as it stands; but I think I've a very good idea what she sang—having seen the reports of the shows she has seen—so of course that made it much better... It is a song from 'Annie Get Your Gun' entitled 'Doing What Comes Naturally'.

One speculates whether Haigh ever did anything naturally, whether his entire life was so unnatural that he was incapable of genuine love and affection, although there is no question that he was fond of Barbara Stephens—'in a brotherly sort of way'. How then did he inspire affection in others?

From the condemned cell Haigh wrote to Dr Yellowlees as follows:

Dear Sir, I would like you to know that I appreciate the personal interest you have taken and the effort you have made on my behalf, even though I cannot agree with your opinion. After all, all the outstanding personalities throughout history have been considered odd: Confucius, Jesus Christ, Julius Caesar, Mahomet, Napoleon and even Hitler; all possessed a greater perception of the infinite and a more lucid understanding of the omniscient mind. I am happy to inform you that my mother, during last week, was able to confirm that my headmistress at the High School and my headmaster at the grammar school both reported that I wasn't a normal boy. How could it be otherwise in the product of an angel and one of the few men who never sinned? I do therefore have the greatest admiration for your greater perception and am grateful to you for your courageous exposition of it. Yours truly, J. G. Haigh.

I asked a man who knew the Haigh family—as far as it was possible for anybody to know the Haigh family—to tell me what he knew about them and the son in particular. He is the man who entrusted me with copies of Haigh's letters to his parents from prison and the death cell. He is the chairman of an important public company and wishes to remain anonymous, but this is what he wrote:

The case was of special interest to me because I had known Haigh for more than thirty years as the gifted son and only child of parents who lived in the village of Outwood, near Wakefield.

'Chink', as Haigh was called, was brought up in an atmosphere which was peculiar to say the least. There was an aloofness in the attitude of his parents which restricted as perhaps it was intended the number of their friends, a restriction which was severely applied to their son.

He had no chums and only on rare occasions was he allowed to take home a boy of his own age, who must belong to a middle-class family, for there was snobbery besides aloofness in the make-up of his parents. My brother, who was a fellow pupil of Haigh at the Wakefield Grammar School, used to call at 'Chink's' home on schooldays for several years and give a certain signal on the doorbell, yet he was never asked inside the house, even when Haigh was not quite ready for school.

The boy had rare gifts of mind and possessed even as a child an acute and precocious intelligence. Whatever may be said in criticism of the severity of his upbringing, with its ultra-religious bias, it is also true that the devotion of his parents was intended to provide their son with scope, both educational and otherwise, for the utilisation of those gifts.

For music, Haigh had a genuine love and he excelled as a pianist long before other and older boys had mastered their five finger exercises. His voice secured for him a choral scholarship at the Grammar School and he was for many years a chorister at Wakefield Cathedral and afterwards at Leeds Parish Church. He had perfect manners and a likeable though at times cheeky disposition and one cannot think that he really missed the normal day to day companionship of other boys.

Despite his gifts and his charm (on appropriate occasions) there was a nasty side to Haigh's character when a boy. He delighted, for instance, to spit upon ascending and descending passengers from the upper deck of the trams on which he travelled to and from the School, and took some trouble when the opportunity presented itself of exposing his private parts to travelling schoolgirls. He seemed to prefer to play a lone hand in boyish pranks and had a flair for the unusual in this direction also.

So there goes the picture of the exemplary schoolboy with shining morning face as seen by his teachers. In comes a picture of a boy spitting down on people and flashing his genitals at schoolgirls, a boy anxious to demonstrate his contempt for people, a boy deriving pleasure from outrageous behaviour, anxious to set at naught all that his parents have instilled into him. In the case of John George Haigh is not the boy father to the man?

Whilst a psychiatrist might be able to deduce from the foregoing some of the causes for a career of crime which began almost as soon as Haigh left school, and eventually brought about his execution for murder a few days after his fortieth birthday, no ordinary observer or contemporary of his earlier life could have dreamt of such possibilities ahead for him.

So writes a man who knew the family as well as anybody could be expected to know the aloof Haighs who considered themselves 'the elect of God'.

There was a heavy fall of snow on Saturday, March 5th, 1949 [writes this man of good will and integrity]. During that morning I received a telephone message from Haigh's father, asking if I would go over to Leeds that afternoon.

Although I had not seen Haigh's parents for years I had been in fairly frequent touch with them on small business matters for many years and for a somewhat lengthy spell had regularly received from them certain religious publications in which they were interested.

I went to Leeds that afternoon in a state of apprehension, not liking the idea that I may be asked to do something for the Haighs in connection with the defence of their son . . .

I found both father and mother well-nigh crushed by the blow which had fallen upon them in their eighties, at a time when, for all they knew, George was a successful man of business in London. They required no practical help from me, They said they wanted someone to talk to, for it seemed that their persistent aloofness had robbed them of a confidant when they were in need of one.

Over a period of three hours or more I was able to piece together some of the happenings of the last few days, from the time when, picking up the morning newspaper from the door-mat Mr Haigh found himself looking at a photograph of his son, who was said to be 'assisting' the Metropolitan police in connection with the disappearance of Mrs Durand-Deacon to the receipt that morning of a letter which he had written from Lewes Gaol, assuring his parents that there was no need for worry or alarm.

'But', said his father, 'the police don't arrest anybody for murder unless they are sure'.

By the time of my first visit to Leeds newspaper speculation had begun to range round the names of a number of missing persons, the Hendersons and the McSwans in particular and it was clear that Haigh's parents, who knew and had corresponded with some of these persons, as they had done with Mrs Durand-Deacon, were beginning to fear that their son had something to do with these other disappearances.

It would take a far more skilful pen than mine to describe the torment of heart and mind in which I left these old people to make my way home in the snow.

This was the first of many visits to Leeds to try and do a little to help them bear their grievous burden, which became heavier as the police court proceedings first, and later the trial, disclosed the enormity of George's actions self-confessed and which were in such vivid contrast to the self-assured and often amusing letters he wrote from the prison throughout his detention.

Haigh's letters were, for the most part, masterly compositions. They evidenced the deepest affection for his parents, and except for the last which he signed 'John George', concluded with expressions of his affection from 'Sonnie'. Occasionally he would make some reference to the proceedings which were being taken against him, and in one letter after the final police court proceedings he referred to the manner in which the prosecution had 'put the parsley round the cod'. For the most part, however, he was content to write of abstruse points of theology and philosophy or go into details on matters mentioned by his mother. One of these, I remember, was the suitable shade of curtains for his bedroom at home, and another the appropriate design and colour of a jumper to be worn by a lady friend.

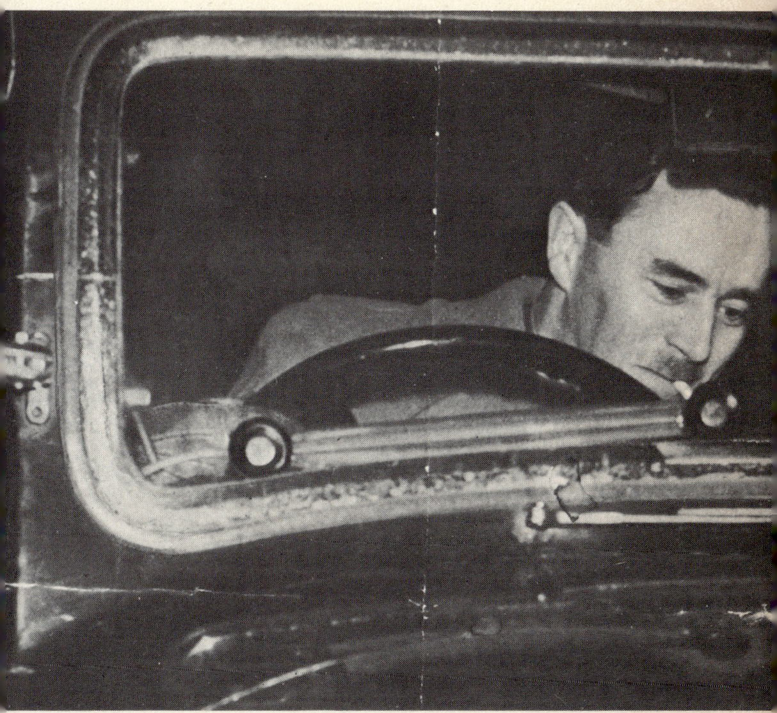

Associated Newspapers

Haigh at the wheel of his Alvis outside the Onslow Court Hotel, South Kensington, in February 1949: the original caption to this news photo described him as 'a friend of the missing widow', and shortly after it was taken he was arrested.

Press Association

Haigh smiling as he leaves the court after being committed to stand trial. He complained bitterly about the irresponsible behaviour of housewives who stampeded to catch a glimpse of him.

LOYAL WEALD OF SUSSEX
OF ODD FELLOWS
NATIONAL DEPOSIT

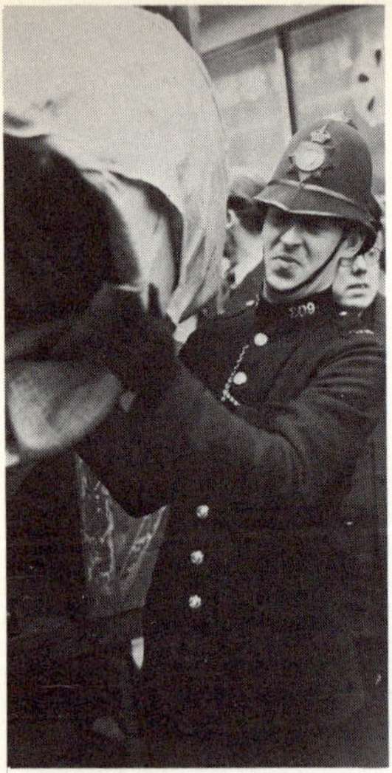

Press Association

Press Association

Press Association

Press Association

(*Above, left*) a policeman brings into court the metal drum in which Haigh dissolved Mrs Durand-Deacon. (*Above, right*) Mrs Constance Lane (*nearest camera*), a friend of Mrs Durand-Deacon who gave evidence at Haigh's trial.
(*Below, left*) Det.-Sgt. Patrick Heslin (*left*) and Divisional Det.-Insp. Shelley Symes (*centre*) at Horsham. (*Below, right*) Dr (now Professor) Keith Simpson leaving Horsham Magistrates' Court after giving evidence (April 1).

replying to this letter, please write on the envelope:— 1

umber 2074 Name Haigh J

BRIXTON Prison

16. 3. 49.

My dear Sophie:

Very many thanks for your kindly and understanding letter: also for the lovely letter which my mother informs me you have sent to her. I hope she is going to meet you. She knows how kind you have been to me and that I dearly love you all.

I face the future with complacency knowing not what man can do: for he still gropes in the darkness and ~~on~~ comprehends not the light; not having learned to drink of the water of life, saying platitudinously that blood is thicker than water and knowing not what it means.

But there is no good in my exposing that thought as nobody ever understands me

Tome will doubtless have told you that I have arranged for patent renewal fees and all matters thereto to be cared for for so long as I am unable to do so personally.

Also the Walpole Investment Trust.

It is with joy that I remember those heavens that I have known in the many happy days that I have spent with you: the most wonderful

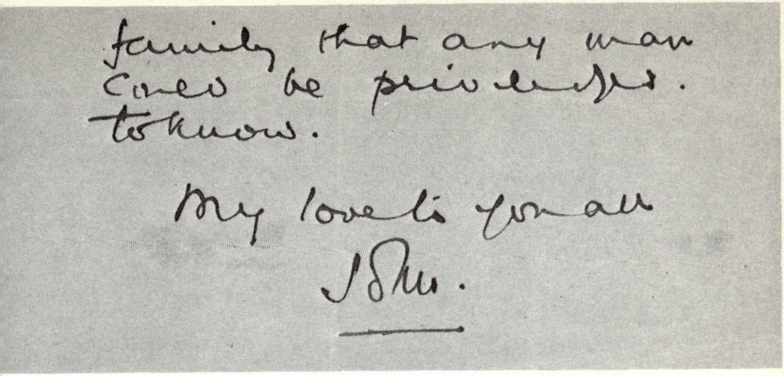

family that any man could be privileged to know.

My love to you all

John.

A letter that Haigh wrote to Mrs Feuerheerd from his cell in Brixton Prison while awaiting trial. 'I face the future with complacency . . .'

On July 20th he wrote to his parents from the death cell in Wandsworth Prison . . .

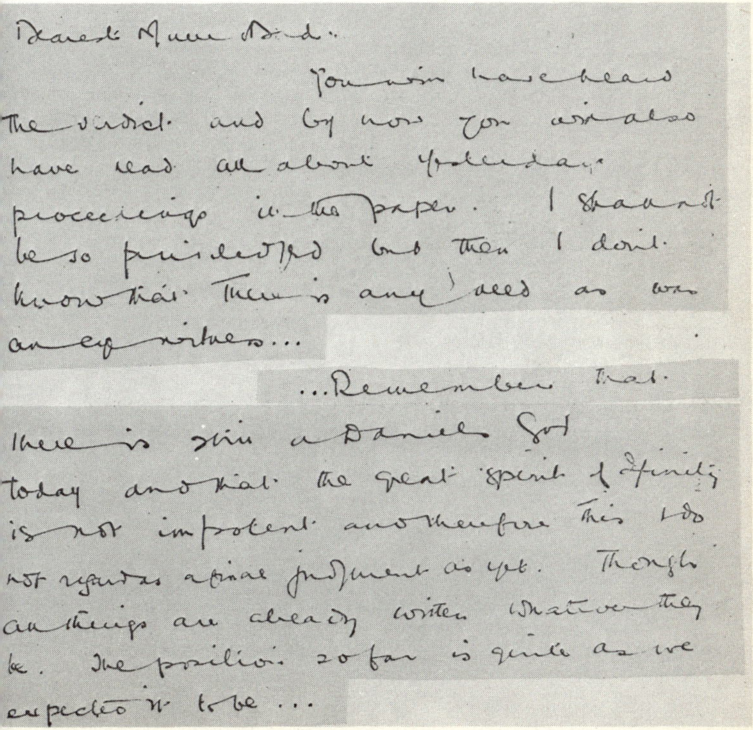

Dearest Mum and Dad.

You will have heard the verdict and by now you will also have read all about yesterday's proceedings in the paper. I shall not be so privileged but then I don't know that there is any need as I was an eye witness...

...Remember that there is still a Daniel Got today and that the great spirit of Infinity is not impotent and therefore this I do not regard as a final judgement as yet. Though all things are already written whatever they be. The position so far is quite as we expected it to be...

and from the same cell he wrote to the pianist Albert Ferber on August 5th . . .

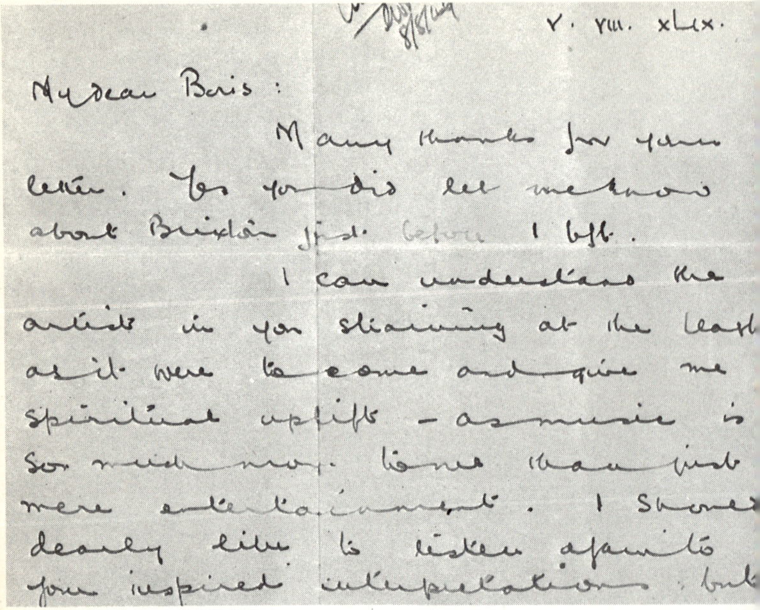

V. VIII. XLIX.

My dear Boris:

Many thanks for your letter. As you did let me know about Brixton just before I left.

I can understand the artist in you straining at the leash as it were to come and give me spiritual uplift – as music is so much more to me than just mere entertainment. I should dearly like to listen again to your inspired interpretations but

and once more to his parents on August 8th . . .

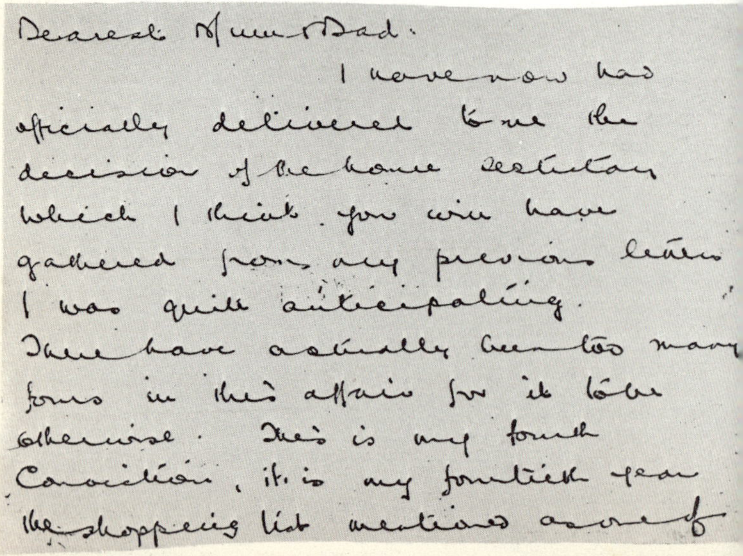

Dearest Mum & Dad:

I have now had officially delivered to me the decision of the home secretary which I think you will have gathered from my previous letters I was quite anticipating. There have actually been too many forms in this affair for it to be otherwise. This is my fourth conviction, it is my fourteenth year the shopping list mentioned as one of

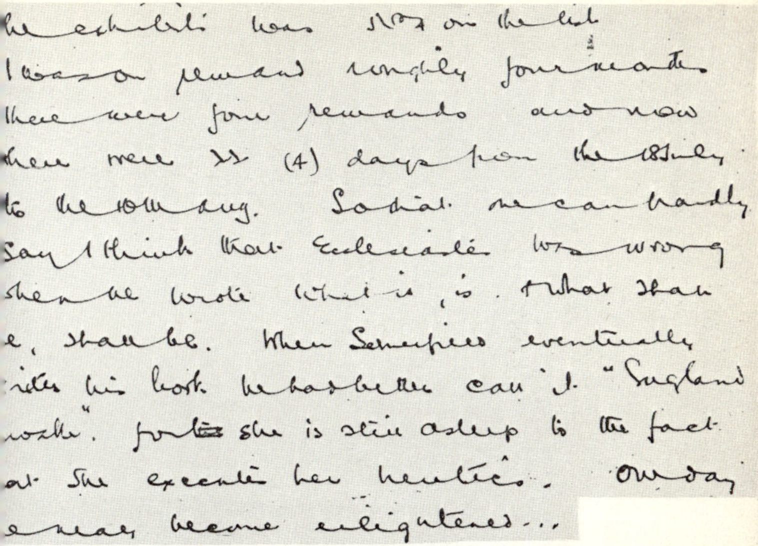
he exhibit was 1107 on the list
I was on remand roughly four months
there were four remands and now
there were 22 (4) days from the 18 July
to the 10th Aug. So that one can hardly
say I think that Ecclesiastes was wrong
when he wrote What is, is. & What shall
be, shall be. When Sempills eventually
writes his book he had better call it "England
Awake". for she is still asleep to the fact
that she executes her heretics. One day
she may become enlightened . . .

Haigh appears more cheerful than ever after sentence of death has been passed. *Press Association*

On the eve of his execution Haigh wrote his last letter to his parents, four pages long.

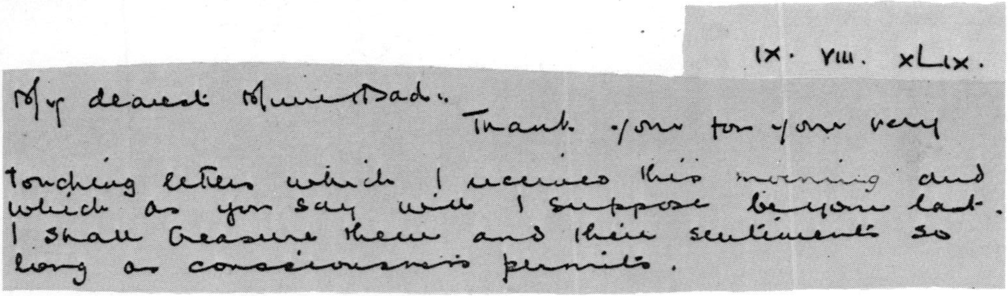

IX. VIII. XLIX.

My dearest Mum & Dad.

Thank you for your very touching letter which I received this morning and which as you say will I suppose be your last. I shall treasure them and their sentiments so long as consciousness permits.

The handwriting perhaps betrays a sense of urgency, but the words are still confident and affectionate . . .

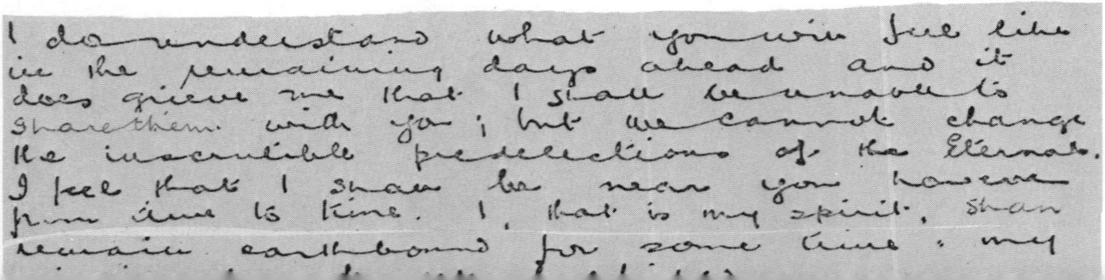

I do understand what you will feel like in the remaining days ahead and it does grieve me that I shall be unable to share them with you; but we cannot change the inscrutible predilections of the Eternal. I feel that I shall be near you however from time to time. I, that is my spirit, shall remain earthbound for some time: my

He closed: 'Please give my love to everybody and thank them on my behalf for their kindly solicitations . . .

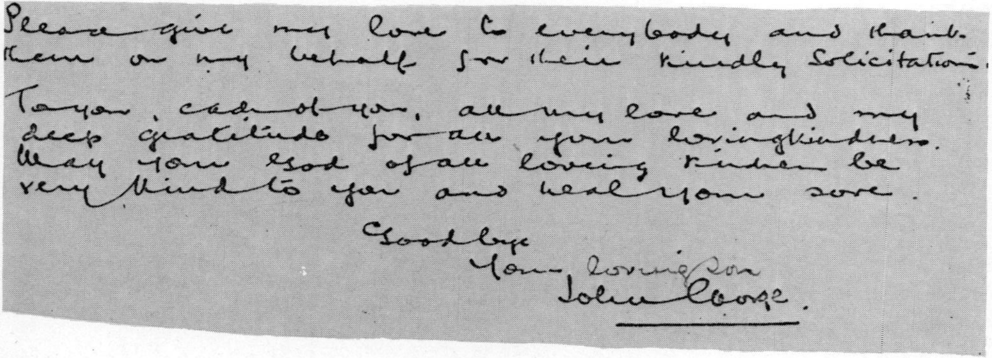
Please give my love to everybody and thank them on my behalf for their kindly Solicitations.

To you, each of you, all my love and my deep gratitude for all your loving kindness. May your God of all loving kindness be very kind to you and heal your sore.

Goodbye

Your loving son

John Coope.

Press Association

Press Association

Press Association

Press Association

(*Top*) eighty-year-old Mr Justice Humphreys on his way to hear the case against Haigh at Lewes Assizes on July 18th. (*Bottom*, *left*) Sir Hartley Shawcross, Q.C., the Attorney-General, on his way to lunch at the White Hart, Lewes, after opening the Crown's case against Haigh. (*Centre*) Sir David Maxwell Fyfe, Counsel for the Defence. (*Right*) Dr Henry Yellowlees, the only witness called for the Defence – for him a painful experience.

As the weeks passed, it seemed as if the spirit of the parents rose through the belief that George would not hang because the prosecution could not produce a body and they were filled with a growing hope that he would be found guilty but insane and sent to Broadmoor.

His father, who maintained all along that 'our George' must be mad, often referred to his son's tenderness of heart, especially for animals and children, and accepted as the explanation of the various crimes George's statement in one of his letters from prison that ever since he was injured about the head in a motor accident which befel him one Friday many months previously, he had been seized at intervals—and always on a Friday—by an uncontrollable force or impulse for evil.

A strange feature . . ., at least it was to me, was the fact that on no occasion did he express a wish to see his parents, and when his mother suggested her willingness to visit him, he put her off with a promise to 'have a word with Eager' (his solicitor) and made no further reference to the matter. His father's explanation of this attitude was probably the right one, that 'our George' would be ashamed to receive his mother in prison and unable to talk to her naturally in the presence of prison warders.

I doubt whether Haigh's father was right in this assumption. Not once in the letters does he evince any sense of shame. He alternates between the boredom of being confined to a cell to an almost grandiose glorying in the importance of his trial, never at a loss for a joke. He never sheds a tear. I find it difficult to believe that Haigh was ever remotely aware of shame.

[Again, according to the friend of the family], Mrs Haigh made many references to George's victims in her conversations with me, for she had met the McSwans and corresponded with Mrs Durand-Deacon. I was given one of that lady's letters to read. In it, she wrote of George's charm and kindness and of his love for her dog, which he had taken with him to Leeds in the previous November, his last visit to his parents.

In our conversation the name of Mrs Henderson cropped up and I was told of an occasion when, according to George in one of his letters home, after lunching with him at the Onslow Court Hotel she had taken him to a shop and bought him two pairs of grey socks. George had then shewn Mrs Henderson the grey socks he was wearing, one of nine pairs knitted by his mother during the previous winter, and his companion had said, 'Well, if I had known you had such lovely hand-knitted socks I wouldn't have wasted my money on you.'

We get a tiny clue to the character of Mrs Haigh in the letter which she dashes off to her son.

'What business has Mrs Henderson to buy you socks?' she asks.

'You must remember, mum,' Haigh wrote back, 'that some people get a lot of pleasure out of making presents to their friends.'

Mrs Haigh shook her head and said, 'I always thought it a strange thing for her to do.'

During his association with the pin-table business of the McSwans, when Haigh self-styled himself their manager, he received a two-day visit from his mother and shewed her round the factory, introducing her to his employers and some of his associates in the business.

When Mrs Haigh got home, she wrote to her son, expressing uneasiness at the sort of people he was mixing with, expressing a hope that he would get away from them.

It was, of course, ludicrous of Mrs Haigh to fear that her son might be contaminated by evil companions. He was an established rogue. He was no weak character in danger of being led astray. Bad companions had no part in luring John George Haigh from the paths of righteousness. He was never on them. His mother and father put him on the road to infamy by their fanaticism of their religious upbringing, their total lack of humanity and human weaknesses, except the worst, pride. It is not difficult to imagine young 'Sonnie' Haigh vowing to spit in the face of society, just as he had spat on the heads of tramcar passengers, vowing to do something quite diabolical and outrageous. He kept his vow.

The anonymous friend of the Haighs recalls the strange events of the final days.

As the time of Haigh's trial drew near, the tone of his letters became more bombastic and they contained frequent and involved references to the part which he thought the Almighty was going to play in the proceedings.

He had chosen his Counsel he said because he was attracted by the christian name of 'David' and believed that he would be capable of dealing with his own Goliath....

During those last three weeks between the sentence and his execution there was no obvious change in the tone of Haigh's letters to his father and mother. He wrote of his 'mission'; that it was not ended, and that it would go on even if 'this envelope', the body, was disposed of according to the will of man.

Haigh had his fortieth birthday in the condemned cell. Two days earlier I had received a note from his mother, who could not bring herself to go out shopping, asking to buy for her a 'suitable' birthday card to send to George and telling me where I might get a good card for 2/6d or 3/–. She could not have set me a more difficult task. I read the words of at least a hundred cards in three or four shops, rejecting the majority which wished 'many happy years ahead' and 'a coming year filled with many joys', sentiments which were neither appropriate nor likely to be helpful to a man who had less than three weeks to live. In the end I bought a dozen cards bearing sentiments of a more restrained and restricted character, from which Mrs Haigh was able to chose one which she considered suitable....

(What sort of birthday card is suitable for a mother to send to a son who is about to be hanged?)

Apart from his dislike of conditions in the condemned cell at Wandsworth, where he wore prison clothes and was under constant observation, Haigh made a few complaints to his parents about prison life at Lewes and Brixton. On one occasion he wrote 'how I hate this sunshine', which he could not enjoy, but otherwise he wrote in approving terms of treatment he received and of the facilities he enjoyed.

His love of sunshine and of the countryside was no doubt genuine. After his committal for trial by the magistrates at Horsham, Haigh was driven back to London. In a letter written to his parents that evening he wrote of his day that 'things went very much as we expected' and described at length a mis-hap on the floor of the police car when he and the policeman to whom he was handcuffed fell over one another and ended up in a heap. . . .

The question of an appeal was considered and Haigh told his parents that there was not to be one, that he was content to leave the matter to 'the authorities', meaning the Home Secretary, and that he was quite happy to leave himself to the 'inevitable!'

On the day before his execution, Prisoner 7663, Haigh, John George, wrote his last letter to his parents:

My dearest Mum & Dad,

Thank you for your very touching letter which I received this morning and which as you say will I suppose be your last. I shall treasure them and the sentiments as long as consciousness permits.

I hardly need tell you that although I found the early theological restrictions oppressive there was much that was very lovely. There was great—in fact, overwhelming kindness and consideration which I remember with much gratitude. In these later years I looked forward with great eagerness to my periodic visits of short duration. How can I possibly tell you how I feel about it and expect you to understand. The richness of anticipation and the pleasure of deciding what I should bring for you and the great joy of presenting it and witnessing the fondness of your reception of it. Of how when I used to leave I used to wish I were just arriving and yet knowing that I should not have wholly enjoyed a protracted stay. But, like yours, my memoirs of the very pleasant days I used to love the walks with dad and the nocturnal chats with mam. How glad I am that I was able to get along last November. I looked forward to that for the whole year.

I have not received the letter from Australia but never mind. Rosemary sent such a sweet little note this morning. You will no doubt get this along with the rest in due course and from them you may find comfort in the sentiments of them. You may tell Mona I also remember her coming when Dad and I were in the garden and I said who on earth's this—obviously sensing danger in the female presence!—and Dad said oh that's your cousin Mona. I also remember it for another special reason. I have often wondered at times whether she remembers it for the same. I wish I could ask her privately.

I do understand what you will feel like in the remaining days ahead and it does grieve me that I shall be unable to share them with you; but we cannot change the inscrutable predictions of the Eternal. I feel sure that I shall be near you however from time to time. I, that is my spirit, shall remain earthbound for some time: my mission is not yet fulfilled.

I referred to the incidence of 'Fours' (?) etc. yesterday. Now do you remember the man at Bradford who your Auntie Georgie went to see. Amongst other things he wrote; there's a great likelihood of bones being broken in the hunting field. This need not necessarily be the cries of joy and hounds of course. And this I think you will agree is not out of keeping with Ecclesiastics and his lot which is written.

Of course if I were to write to you of my thoughts I should need a book—or more.

Mr Somerfield came again this afternoon and we had a very pleasant half hour. He will be collecting my goods and chattels from Eagle and from the Yard and will in due course be bringing them to you. I hope you enjoy the Phillips Radio. I found it very satisfactory without interference used with the earth.

There is a built in aerial as well as the plug for an outside one—naturally the latter is in storage. You can get America direct towards the left hand side of the short wave band in the evening.

My typewriter I know you will not use and this with its accessories I have asked Somerfield to take to Ba.

You will have heard from the Chaplain* in due course. He has spent at least an hour with me each evening and we have had very pleasant chats together. You will remember him sending me Christmas cards after I left Dartmoor.

He was very touched by your recent letters. I have no doubt that should he ever come to Leeds he will come to see you.

Please give my love to everybody and thank them on my behalf for their kindly solicitations.

To you, each of you, all my love and my deep gratitude for all your loving kindness. May your God of all loving kindness be very kind to you and heal your sore.

Goodbye,

Your loving son,

John George.

In this, his last letter to his parents from the condemned cell, Haigh signs himself John George, underlining the signature. Why he does this instead of signing himself 'Sonnie', as was his custom, is inexplicable. He does however add a postscript which he signs 'Sonnie' and this is added late at night:

P.S.

9.30 p.m. The Chaplain has had a very beautiful note from Hugh R. Norton (Cathedral) who writes to have the privilege of consoling with: I have told the Chaplain that I am sure you will appreciate this.

Sonnie.

Well, that is Haigh's last letter to his parents, written on the eve of his execution. Can any judge or jurist, any psychiatrist,

* The late Rev. B. H. Powell.

say that it is the letter of a totally sane man? It is a truly intriguing document and not the least ironic aspect of it is that it was read for censorship and initialled by a prison officer on the following day*, August 10th, 1949, *after* Haigh had been hanged at 9 a.m. precisely, in the near record time of eleven seconds between condemned cell and execution shed. In prison not even a dead man can tell any tales not approved by the Home Office.

Hundreds of people who had nothing better to do on that August morning, including women with children, surged forward to read the official certification of death by hanging when it was posted on the door of Wandsworth Prison, a few minutes later.

'I, Leslie Ingham Shyder, the Surgeon of His Majesty's Prison of Wandsworth, hereby certify that I this day examined the body of John George Haigh on whom Judgment of Death was this day executed in the said Prison; and in that examination I found that the said John George Haigh was dead. This 10th day of August 1949.'

* In the *Notable British Trials* series the date of Haigh's execution is erroneously given as August 6th.

A Lady in the Evening of her Life

Mrs Olive Henrietta Helen Olivia Robarts Durand-Deacon, who was Haigh's ninth victim according to his own confession, was a Christian Scientist and an active member of the Francis Bacon Society, the people who believe that Shakespeare's works were written by Bacon. This in itself is a pointer to the fact that she was inclined to be gullible, ready to embrace or join any movement that was not quite orthodox.

A widow of a colonel in the Glorious Gloucesters, she had an income of about a thousand pounds a year. Previous to moving into the Onslow Court she had lived at the Langham Hotel, now used as overspill offices by the British Broadcasting Corporation. At the age of sixty-nine she weighed fourteen stone. Sir Hartley Shawcross, as he was then, described her aptly as 'a lady in the evening of her life.'

She had no reason to think that her life's evening would be terminated so violently by the charming man who occupied the next table to her at Onslow Court, the man who had accompanied her to Foyle's literary luncheons, the man who ingratiated himself with other aged ladies in the hotel by obtaining additional eggs and butter for them, the poor rich old dears not realising that the nice Mr Haigh was obtaining these postwar luxuries by using the ration books of the McSwans and the Hendersons, all of whom he had murdered. They were self-indulgent old ladies and asked no awkward questions, any more than Mrs Durand-Deacon asked the origin of the crocodile handbag she bought from Haigh for ten pounds, a real bargain. She had no reason to suspect that it had been the property of Mrs Rosalie Henderson who had been murdered in the workshop at Crawley where she too was destined to come to a grisly and shocking end.

'I shot her in the back of the neck,' Haigh confessed. 'And, as with all the others, made an incision and drew a glass of blood. One thing I remember vividly, she was wearing a crucifix around her neck. It gave me infinite delight to stamp it into the ground.'

Whether this part of Haigh's confession is true is questionable. No such crucifix was found by the police when the premises at Leopold Road, Crawley, were subjected to a very thorough search. His victim was wearing pearls and other jewellery, together with a Persian lamb coat. She was not carrying the handbag she had bought from Haigh but a red plastic one.

Haigh stripped Mrs Durand-Deacon of her jewellery and divested her of the Persian lamb coat before putting her body into the non-corrosive drum.

Having achieved this, an operation involving two hours of hard labour, Haigh felt in need of sustenance. So he got in his car and drove off to Ye Olde Ancient Prior's restaurant in Crawley Square where he had eggs on toast and a coffee.

Everybody who knew Haigh said that he was a most fastidious man. Nobody could accuse him of being squeamish.

Having satisfied his hunger he drove back to his 'workshop'. If we are to believe his story that he drank a glass of Mrs Henderson's blood before he went off for eggs and toast it is most remarkable that he was not physically sick.

I am told that it is pathologically impossible to extract half a pint of blood from a dead person, unless a syringe is used. Haigh never used one.

One cannot help arriving at the conclusion that this part of Haigh's confession was a figment of imagination, so lurid that it might convince a jury that he was mad and not responsible for his actions, but believing himself to be under the influence of a mystic power outside himself.

Returning to the 'workshop' in Leopold Road, Haigh found he had left the door open. Any chance passer-by could have wandered in and seen the body of Mrs Durand-Deacon in the drum.

Haigh's statement at Chelsea Police Station on the night of February 28th, 1949, was made to Divisional Detective-Inspector Shelley Symes and witnessed by Superintendent T. Barrott:

> Statement of John George Haigh, age 39 years, an independent engineer of the Onslow Court Hotel, Queen's Gate, SW 7 who saith:
>
> I have been cautioned that I am not obliged to say anything unless I wish to do so, but whatever I say will be taken down in writing and my be given in evidence. (J.G.H.)
>
> I have already made some statements to you about the disappearance of Mrs Durand-Deacon. I have been worried about the matter and fenced about in the hope that you would not find out about it. The truth is that we left the Hotel together in my car. She was inveigled into going to Crawley by me in view of her interest in artificial finger nails. Having taken her into the store room at Leopold Road I shot her in the back of her head whilst she was examining some paper for use as finger nails. Then I went out to the car and fetched in a drinking glass and made an incision, I think with a penknife, in the side of the throat, and collected a glass of blood, which I then drank. Following that I removed the coat she was wearing, a Persian lamb, and the jewellery, rings, necklace, ear-rings and cruciform and put her in a 45 gallon (it was 40) tank. I then filled the tank up with sulphuric acid by means of a stirrup pump from a carboy. I then left it to re-act. I should have said in between putting her in the tank and pumping in the acid I went round to the Ancient Priors for a cup of tea. Having left the tank to re-act, I brought the jewellery and revolver into the car and left the coat on the bench. I went to the 'George'*

* The George Inn, where he had spent a convivial Christmas.

for dinner and I remember I was late, about 'ninish'. I then came back to town and returned to the hotel about half-past ten. I put the revolver back into the square hat box.

The following morning I had breakfast and as I have already said, discussed the disappearance of Mrs Durand-Deacon with the waitress and Mrs Lane. I eventually went back to Crawley via Putney where I sold her watch en route at a jewellers in the High Street for ten pounds. I took this watch from her at the same time as the other jewellery. At Crawley I called in to see how the re-action in the tank had gone on. It was not satisfactorily completed, so I went on to Horsham, having picked up the coat and put it in the back of the car. I called at Bull's, the jewellers, for a valuation of the jewellery, but Mr Bull was not in. I returned to town and on the way dropped in the coat at the 'Cottage Cleaners' at Reigate. On Monday I returned to Crawley to find the re-action almost complete, but a piece of fat and bone was still floating on the sludge. I emptied off the sludge with a bucket and tipped it on the ground opposite the shed, and pumped a further quantity of acid into the tank to decompose the remaining fat and bone. I went to Horsham again and had the jewellery valued, ostensibly for Probate. It was valued at just over £130....

I returned to Horsham on Tuesday and sold the jewellery for what was offered at a purchase price of £100. Unfortunately, the jewellers had not got that amount of money and could only give me £60. I called back for the £40 the next day. On the Tuesday I returned to Crawley and found decomposition complete and emptied the tank off. I would add that on the Monday I found that the only thing which the acid had not attacked was the plastic handbag and I tipped this out with the sludge. On the Tuesday when I completely emptied the tank, I left it outside in the yard....

Before I put the handbag in the tank I took from it the cash, about thirty shillings, and her fountain pen and kept these. I tipped the rest into the tank with the bag. The fountain pen is still in my room....

The ration books and clothing coupons in the names of McSwan and Henderson are the subject of another story....

He talked into the small hours, fortified by cups of tea and cigarettes, apparently quite unperturbed, correcting himself as he went along, anxious to get events in the right sequence.

It was past two o'clock on the morning of March 1st when Haigh eventually signed his statement, having been at Chelsea Police Station since 4.15 p.m. on the previous day. He was then taken to Horsham, Sussex, where he was formally charged and thence conveyed to Lewes Prison.

Tuesday of that week happened to be Shrove Tuesday. He demanded pancakes and got them, although there is no record of the crazy housewives he so deplored racing along the winding High Street to be first at the prison gates with them.

On March 4th Haigh asked Detective-Inspector Webb to come and see him at Lewes. Having already confessed to the murder of Mrs Durand-Deacon, Dr and Mrs Henderson as well as the McSwan family, he now confessed to three other murders, a youth called Max, a shop girl from Hammersmith and another girl from Eastbourne. The details he gave about these murders were vague in the extreme, so much so that the police were inclined to the view that Haigh had invented three phantom victims.

The first cuckoo was heard. Mauve and white crocus tips peeped out from the greensward. March hares were faster than the two-year-olds on Lewes race-course gallops and soon it was Easter.

> Dear Mum and Dad, [Haigh wrote] Hasn't it been a wonderful week-end. Much too hot and pleasant to be here. Ba came on Saturday and looked absolutely cooked. I'm sure it can't last. I've never known such an Easter.... I am very pleased indeed to hear how kind the neighbours are in their inquiries.... I guess Mum would have liked to see the Easter Parade in Hyde Park yesterday. All the new Dolly Vardens! Be brave and remember David!

Two days later he wrote,

> Well, glorious Easter weather is holding out. Wasn't it wonderful? Most depressing in here, of course. I'd rather have dull weather in here.

In prison on a charge of murder, having confessed to nine, he then goes on to regale his Mum and Dad with a money-making idea for saving people from accidental death by coal gas poisoning.

> I've read one or two cases accounts recently about people being found dead in gassed rooms. I got the inspiration for its prevention last night and by early morning had solved the problem.
>
> Simple, cheap and it will be impossible to leave the gas on without it being alight. If it goes out through shortage of gas then the tap will turn off automatically. . . . If eventually I get out of this pickle there are ten million homes in England. . . . Now work that out for yourself at a penny royalty per tap.

Well, as we know, Haigh did not 'get out of this pickle' and his device for saving people from accidental—or even intentional—death by gas poisoning was never patented. He did not live to get a penny royalty on every gas tap in the country, but one cannot help wondering what sort of man could occupy his thoughts upon such a scheme whilst incarcerated and awaiting trial for murder.

It is a strange anomaly that persons on minor charges can be placed alongside murderers in the so-called prison hospital if a magistrate has ordered that they should be kept under observation, for a week or longer, before coming to a decision about their guilt or innocence. Such a man was ex-Sergeant Major A. G. Smith who was sent to Brixton for observation because of an outburst of temper he gave vent to in Marylebone Police Court.

'I had served 18 years with the colours,' he told me. 'I was in business as a road haulage contractor and I was summoned to appear at Marylebone on April 6th, 1949, for procuring, aiding and abetting one of my drivers to drive a lorry while disqualified.

'It was a technical offence and normally would have resulted in a fine—as it was eventually—but unfortunately I lost my temper with the prosecuting counsel and the Magistrate ordered me to be detained for a medical report and I was taken by Black Maria to Brixton Prison Hospital. I was in Ward A, ostensibly under the observation of Dr Mathieson and other doctors in the company of John George Haigh, Frederick Cooper and Sidney Archibald Chamberlain, all murderers awaiting trial.

'Haigh told me a great deal about himself and his crimes and the story he told me was not the story his counsel told in court, nor even the story he 'spilled' to the police. It struck me he was preparing an insanity defence which would be substantiated by confessions of blood and urine drinking.

'There was also this man Atkinson in A Ward who had been in Broadmoor and Haigh plied him with questions, getting all the dope from him about symptoms of lunacy, among which blood and urine drinking are included.

'Haigh was by no means "nutty as a fruit cake". He talked and joked freely, prepared to wager that the other two murderers would hang and he would go to Broadmoor and be released in between five and ten years.

'I saw Haigh twice a day in his cell, the door of which was always open, though a barrier prevented the murderers from getting out onto the A Ward landing, except when we were taken out for exercise.

We walked two abreast in the exercise yard and Haigh was always the smartest of the prisoners under what is called medical observation, although most of the so-called observation was carried out by the "screws", while the so-called medical orderlies were really red-band prisoners.

'As prisoners on remand we all wore our own clothes, but Haigh stood out a mile, despite his small stature. Fit for the "Tailor and Cutter", he was. I reckon if they'd given a prize for the best dressed prisoner of the year, Haigh would have won it hands down. Neat as a new pin, he was, his shoes an advert for Cherry Blossom and always carrying or wearing his lemon kid gloves, his hair shining like patent leather.

'He was a generous bloke. He used to get boxes of fifty cigarettes sent in to him and would hand them around freely and fags in prison were like gold dust. He could have sold them, but he said he was above that kind of petty trading.

'Because of the *Daily Mirror* case, he used to say that it was impossible for any twelve men in this country—or any other country—to form an impartial jury.

'Then we were all sent in a van to Maudsley Hospital, Denmark Hill, to have our brains tested. Me on a minor technical charge alongside these murderers.'

Haigh wrote to his parents about his excursion, under escort, to have his 'brain tested' at Maudsley Hospital, and could not resist joking about it:

'With all those gadgets attached to the head, it was rather like having a permanent wave.'

Ex-Sergeant Major A. G. Smith declared that when Haigh talked to him about murdering Mrs Durand-Deacon, he said, 'When I shot the old woman I felt it was my mother I was killing.'

This was a remarkable statement. It is not likely that Smith invented it. In his letters home, Haigh appeared to show affection for his parents. To doctors he described his mother as 'an angel', but did he really feel that way about her? Is there not a note of mockery and almost spiteful railery in some of his letters, when read between the lines?

Mrs Haigh, judging by photographs of her, was something of an old frump. She wore frightful bonnets and yet her darling 'Sonnie' writes from prison that he guesses Mum would have enjoyed the Easter Parade in Hyde Park and all the Dolly Vardens.

One cannot think of a spectacle less likely to attract this eighty-year-old woman who scorned all earthly pleasures, despised her more fun-loving neighbours and considered her husband and herself 'the elect of God'. Haigh himself must have realised the crushing blow he had brought upon his parents in their old age, the spiritual torment they suffered under the dire affliction he had brought upon them, but rarely does he offer words of consolation; rarely a hint of contrition, nothing to lift up their hearts. Rather does he treat the dreadful situation as a huge joke, recounting incidents that made him 'hoot with mirth'.

Dr Noël C. Browne told me, 'Apart from normal personality development which occurs in us all, I doubt whether Haigh was the victim of any drastic change of character, transforming him from a sweet little boy into a cold-blooded murderer. All his life Haigh played a role. He adopted this role as a 'charmer' by way of a defensive mechanism against the strictures of his parents whom he quite possibly hated, despite his letters expressing filial love. He pretended to return their affection, an affection which lacked warmth, because it was more devotional than devoted, more religious than human. Although he wrote them affectionate letters from prison and the death cell, it is possible that secretly he gloated over the misery he had brought upon them remembering the misery they had unconsciously inflicted on him as a child.

'When his narrow-minded parents permitted the young Haigh to escape from the grim confines of their Plymouth Brethren home to sing in the incense-laden atmosphere of Wakefield Cathedral, with its colourful ritual, he enjoyed the new-found freedom but found he was not accepted by the other boys.

'It is not surprising that he grew up hating humanity (with few exceptions), although disguising this hatred under a charm which he had cultivated to such an extent that it became not second nature, but superficially a very real nature. Nearly all mass murderers are self-contained to a degree of callousness and utter disregard of what society deems to be right or wrong.

'Whether or not Haigh committed six or nine murders is comparatively immaterial. One thing is certain, the victims who suffered most cruelly in the end were his own parents.'

What is one to make of a man who writes to his mother from prison, telling her to drink her own urine? She had confided that she was suffering from a gallstone ailment. Haigh wrote back:

'I will ask Mr Baker(?) about the gall stones for you,—but you know the cure alright—but like so many people I have no doubt revolt against the idea—however, you shouldn't you know for it is laid down for you in your own Law Book, Proverbs V 15: "Drink water out of thine own cistern."

'Anyway whoever has the trouble you speak of tell them to try the right cure. They may not fancy the idea (a revulsion born of hypocrisy) but I can assure them of cure. It's no worse than Epsom.'

He continues on the same theme in another letter, but apparently to be applied externally, 'I once thought I might be telling Doreen something new but K— had used the same remedy for his patients and she herself had been taught it by the Mother Superior of her Convent for Curing Chilblains.

'Mind you K— was very clever. He had his own cure for Boils which was really revolting (but then his patients never knew of it) but the boils never returned.'

A few days later he writes, 'Glad you like your bird sanctuary so much. It's one of those things which goes on giving pleasure always. A very good idea wasn't it? . . .

'Ba came on Saturday. She is getting quite an old woman. At least she's losing her memory! Went into a shop the other day for something at 27s put £2 on the counter and forgot to pick up the change and didn't realise it until she got home!'

The very next day Haigh writes in an entirely different tone, derisory of the very people who visited him.

Dear Mum and Dad,

All these people who come to see me with their amusing little theories (which includes the doctors here) I can't help but pity them. Those who come from outside even who say they come to help if possible are so very pitiable: like blind leaders of the blind. For there are more things in the heavens and on earth that they know of. . . .

I'm glad that Ba told you I was bright and cheerful for that is how I am.

We have each a mission to fulfil and as you say only one life to live but it depends on what one means by one life. Physical death does not put an end to that life for we come back again to continue our work, for it must be accomplished. . . .

The wind is in the East today so a bit nippy; but it's nice and fine.

Haigh's letters do not exactly reveal him as one of the world's most profound philosophers, but they are possibly more revealing than the encephalograph examination which he underwent at Maudsley Hospital—which he likened to 'having a permanent wave'.

They do reveal one truth, however. He had no pity for himself any more than he had for his victims.

It was the late Sir David Henderson who wrote of psychopaths: 'The individuals who form this group constitute the biggest, most serious and most controversial medico-legal and social problem . . . they fail to appreciate reality, they are fickle, changeable, lack persistence of effort and are unable to profit by experience or punishment. They are dangerous when frustrated . . . on the surface they can behave as ordinary, likeable, attractive human beings, but they harbour in their inner depths instinctive forces which, on occasions, overwhelm them.'

I cannot imagine anybody disputing that Haigh came under the above category in more respects than one, as indeed did Neville Heath and possibly Donald Hume, each one coldly calculating, each one inordinately vain, but differing in the pattern of their heinous offences. All their crimes were horrific; the wiliest and luckiest of the trio being Hume.

The ordinary honest, decent citizen is naturally appalled by the monstrous crimes committed by Haigh for profit and possibly pleasure. This is no apologia for Haigh, but it has been abundantly proved in recent military history that the same ordinary, decent citizen can be trained to carry out equally diabolical acts in the name of patriotism, nationalism or liberty, and that he will carry it out not only without a qualm or revulsion, but almost with the elated feeling of doing his duty.

So once more we come back to Dr Noël C. Browne's theory:

'Given a different upbringing, Haigh might well have become an RAF pilot bombing Dresden. In which case he would have gone down in history as a hero instead of a monster.'

Haigh was not trained to commit his revolting crimes. He trained himself, experimented with field mice in jars of acid before he tried his formula out on human beings. To him people were of no more account than the creatures who succumbed to his experiments.

He liked to consider himself a perfectionist and he had no more regard for his own life than that of Mrs Durand-Deacon, Dr and Mrs Henderson, or the McSwans.

Haigh is the only murderer in the annals of British crime who actually applied to have a rehearsal of his own execution.

I cannot believe that this was part of an act to feign insanity. There would have been no point in it. The date of his execution was already fixed. There had been no Appeal and the Home Office had decided there was no reason to rescind the ultimate penalty.

'My weight is deceptive,' said Haigh. 'I have a light springy tread and I would not like there to be a hitch.'

Haigh was reassured by Major A. C. N. Benke, Governor of Wandsworth, that this was not likely to happen and that the executioner never made any miscalculations.

'I still think there ought to be a try-out,' Haigh replied.

His request was not granted. And there was no hitch.

Two months later Major Benke was giving evidence before the Royal Commission on Capital Punishment.

'I would not say that the mental state of the average murderer is worse than that of any other cases we get. Murderers are drawn from the general population of the country.'

Asked whether executioners were easy to get, the Major replied, 'Not easy to get, but I believe there are a tremendous number of applicants for the job. It is not easy to get the right man. Great care is taken that only the right man is picked.

'A man who wants to be an executioner must be in a class by himself and I cannot answer for him. The executioners who have attended my prison have not shown any sign of brutality in the carrying out of executions or afterwards. I have not found one executioner who has not taken his job with decorum.'

Major Benke denied that executions caused an atmosphere of extreme tension at prisons where they were carried out.

'Prisoners as a class are self-centred and are little concerned with the fate of others. There is a section of the prison population which treats the affair with callous levity.

I don't think that many experienced prison officers would agree with that bland assertion. Anyway, John George Haigh paid the penalty for his crimes before the prison clock had finished striking nine on the morning of August 10th. Perhaps he was the only one of Wandsworth's prison population who did treat the 'affair with callous levity'.

Highlights of the Trial

It was the Reverend Sydney Smith who wrote of Judges: 'Some have been selected for flexible politics—some are passionate—some are in a hurry—some are violent churchmen—some resemble ancient females—some have the gout—some are eighty years old—some are blind, deaf and have lost their power of smelling.'

Mr Justice Travers Humphreys was eighty-two years of age, the oldest judge in England, but none of the infirmities of senile decay could be attributed to him. He did not have to cup a hand to his ear to listen to the evidence. His face was lined like a crumpled brief but his eyes were bright and darting. He had certainly not lost his sense of smell. In fact, he was ever on the alert to smell an attestational rat.

Born in 1867, educated at Shrewsbury and Trinity Hall, Cambridge, called to the Bar in 1889, knighted in 1925; prosecutor of Browne and Kennedy, the murderers of PC Gutteridge; a judge since 1928, he had never had a verdict reversed or misdirected a jury in his innumerable summings-up. He had seen Crippen in the dock, Oscar Wilde, Bywaters and Thompson, Roger Casement, Leopold Harris and Horatio Bottomley. Now he was to try John George Haigh.

Facially, he had one feature that was disconcerting to counsel, prisoners and witnesses alike. He had a pouting lower lip that gave an illusory impression that he didn't believe a word of what he was listening to. In fact, he was painstakingly scrupulous to the extent of using different coloured pencils to take down the evidence of different witnesses, so that there was no fear of getting his notes confused.

Towards the end of the preliminary proceedings at Horsham, where the behaviour of the stampeding women outside the Court had so infuriated Haigh, application was made that the trial should be heard at the Central Criminal Court in London, although the alleged murder of Mrs Durand-Deacon had occurred in Sussex. The reason put forward by Haigh's counsel was that the next Sussex Assizes at Lewes were not due to commence until three months later. Moreover, most of the witnesses being called by the prosecution came from London.

Mr E. G. Robey, son of the music hall star George Robey, raised eyebrows in a way reminiscent of his father's expression in 'I stopped, I looked and I listened', but made no objection, although he did warn the magistrates that a strong line was sometimes taken at the Old Bailey by judges against cases from county assizes sent to London.

That is exactly what happened. Haigh was committed for trial at the Old Bailey, but on April 27th Sir David Maxwell Fyfe applied to have the trial postponed because the defence was not ready.

In view of the fact that Sir David intended to call only one witness for the defence, Dr Yellowlees, it was a surprise application. The prosecution was calling over thirty witnesses and was ready to proceed. Why was the defence not ready? This has never been explained.

As Mr Robey had anticipated, Sir Travers Humphreys took 'a strong line', refusing even to hear the case in London.

'An application has been made to postpone the trial on this capital offence until the next session of this Court,' he said. 'My view is that that application can only be made as a result of a misunderstanding of the law as it exists, and the practice as it often exists. This case has nothing whatever to do with the Central Criminal Court. The indictment before me is a charge of murder in Sussex. Haigh was arrested at Horsham on March 2nd, nearly two months ago. The duty of the Horsham magistrates was to commit Haigh for trial at the next Sussex Assizes. This person is entitled in law to a jury of Sussex persons. This Court is here ready to try him, but now, at the last moment, the Court is told that the defence, which must have said from committal that they were perfectly willing, are not ready for trial. This case is a Sussex case and should be tried in Sussex as is the normal course, and now application is made that I should postpone until the next sitting of this Court.'

The pouting lower lip became as prominent as an unpeeled prawn as the Judge continued, 'Unfortunately, of late years, the idea has grown up that the Central Criminal Court is a sort of dumping ground for trials from all over the country. There still remains in this country the law of venue. This man is entitled to be tried by a Sussex jury, which is a very strong reason for not sending the case away from the proper court to some alien court.

'I hope that in future if such applications are made they will be refused. The Central Criminal Court remains the Assize Court for the City of London and the Central Criminal Court district, as defined in the Act of Parliament—the County of Middlesex, the administrative County of London and certain parts of Essex, Kent and Surrey. It has its own jurisdiction, its own work—and very, very hard work. There is no ground for thinking that it should be used as a place where any serious case committed for trial might be sent to be tried although the jurors of London have nothing to do with the case. It is for that reason I cannot accede to postponing the case until the next session of the Central Criminal Court....

'I refuse that application, but in order that the accused may not say he has been required to stand his trial at a time when he was not ready, in the rather vague language of counsel, because he was discussing with some eminent scientists some question or other, I will remit this case to be tried at the place it should never have left. The indictment will go back to the County of Sussex and he will be tried at the next Lewes Assizes.'

In his eighty-second year he might be, but nobody could say that Sir Travers Humphreys was resembling an ancient female or to be 'in a hurry'. If he had acceded to the application, Haigh's trial could still have been heard much sooner than it was, six weeks earlier in fact than the opening of the Sussex Summer Assizes at Lewes.

No criticism can be levelled at the Judge for his decision. Sir David Maxwell Fyfe was hereinafter to be known as 'David the Unready'.

Nevertheless, perhaps only Sir Travers Humphreys in his eighty-second year could have scathingly referred to the Central Criminal Courts, commonly known the 'Old Bailey' as a 'sort of dumping ground for criminal trials from all over the country' and as 'an alien court'. The very phraseology suggests more than a note of exacerbation in the Judge's mind, implying that he was not inclined to look benevolently on the case for the defence of Haigh. In plain truth, he was distinctly 'rattled', and no judge should allow himself to be in that frame of mind.

Even more surprising is the venerable Judge's observation that Haigh was arrested in Horsham, Sussex. In fact, he was arrested outside the Onslow Court Hotel when he stepped out of his car by Detective-Inspector Webb on the instructions of Divisional Detective-Inspector Shelley Symes. It is true that Detective-Inspector Webb did not tell Haigh 'You're under arrest', but invited him to Chelsea Police Station as a formality—'it won't take a minute'. In fact, it took many hours and there Haigh made his confession of guilt and was held in custody.

Another strange observation made by Sir Travers Humphreys, an observation which he reiterated, was 'that this man is entitled in law to a jury of Sussex persons'. The inference to be drawn from the octogenarian judge's remark could only be interpreted as meaning that the accused would benefit in some way by having a Sussex jury: as opposed to a London jury.

One person who was not in the least dismayed by the learned Judge's decision was the prisoner, John George Haigh.

> Dear Mum and Dad, [he wrote]. At last I've seen the Old Bailey now. I was surprised at its modern aspect. I always imagined it to be a terribly dreary, dark old place, like some old churches with high pews. But it is quite modern architecturally; rather like a large committee room.
>
> I think Humphreys was very stupid—in a way perhaps understandably at his age,—since he was ready (willing) to try the case at this session, there's no reason why he shouldn't have put it off until the next one in May. But it's quite obvious he loves playing to the gallery. All that he said in 28 minutes could have been said in half a minute—'No, application not granted, the application must go to Lewis.' (*sic*)
>
> When he says the Central Criminal Court is overburdened, I'm not surprised [Haigh continued]. It's overburdened with profound verbosity. However, in spite of his age he was cunning enough not to refuse postponement. That would have left a nice loophole. In fact, I was hoping he would drop that brick.
>
> Tata for now,
>
> Your loving Sonnie.

What John George Haigh did not realise, at the time of this letter, was that when he was eventually arraigned at Lewes he would be facing the same 'cunning' Judge.

To those of us who were privileged to watch this unique trial on that sunny Monday morning, following a Sunday of thunder, lightning and torrential rain, it appeared to open on an exceptionally quiet note. There were no histrionics as might have been evident in the more flamboyant days of Sir Patrick Hastings and Sir Edward Marshall Hall.

There was no doubt that the prosecution had left no stone or particle of bone unturned. Besides more than thirty witnesses called for the Crown there were fifty-six exhibits, ranging from Mrs Durand-Deacon's upper and lower dentures to a hairpin.

The witnesses for the prosecution amounted to as formidable an array of decent, honest citizens as one could imagine. There was Mrs Mabel Marriott, part-time employee of the Cottage Cleaners, Reigate, who identified the Persian lamb coat that Haigh had brought in for cleaning. There was Haigh's bank manager. There was Hannah Caplan, book-keeper at the George Hotel, Crawley, who testified that she saw Haigh enter the hotel with Mrs Durand-Deacon, on the afternoon of that lady's disappearance.

'Where did she go?' Counsel asked.

'To the ladies cloakroom.'

'And did Haigh go to the gent's cloakroom?'

'Yes.'

'How long were they in the hotel?'

'He about a minute, and she about two minutes.'

Witness said she saw Haigh and Mrs Durand-Deacon drive off in his car, and that Haigh returned to the hotel alone about half-past nine, going into the dining room.

'No questions,' said Sir David Maxwell Fyfe.

Watching and listening to the trial one could not help coming to the conclusion that Sir David did indeed have something up the sleeve of his black silk gown, so quietly confident did he seem when declining to cross-examine the witnesses for the prosecution, repeating time and time again, 'No questions'. It became almost monotonous.

It wasn't until the second and final day of the trial that Sir David produced his solitary witness, the eminent Dr Yellowlees, in an effort to show that the accused was insane at the time of committing the act charged against him, so as not to be responsible in law for what he did.

It did seem to me at the time that the learned Judge was not disposed to allow the eminent doctor a fair crack of the judicial whip. Dr Yellowlees was entitled to the same courtesy as that accorded the host of witnesses for the prosecution. This was not always apparent, and the jury could not have been uninfluenced by Mr Justice Humphreys's scarcely concealed antagonism.

Before Sir Hartley Shawcross got to his feet to begin his deadly cross-examination, the Judge himself was weighing in with questions and comment, as of course he was perfectly entitled to do, but it seemed to me that the questions and comment were not so much designed to clarify the evidence in the minds of the jury as to discredit it.

Dr Yellowlees had been giving evidence about Haigh's state of mind before and after committing the murder, when Mr Justice Humphreys intervened: 'He told you that he took steps to avoid detection afterwards because he knew quite well that to kill a person was a crime?'

Dr Yellowlees: 'Yes, I think he used the phrase punishable by law.'

'Very well, because he knew that to kill a person was punishable by law?' the Judge persisted.

Dr Yellowlees: 'Yes, and he added that of course it did not apply in his case.'

'What did not apply in his case?' Mr Justice Humphreys asked.

'What I have just said, that murder being punishable by law did not apply to him.'

'Does that suggest he is not amenable to the law?'

'Yes, certainly.'

'Why was he not amenable to the law?'

'Because he says he is working under the guidance and in harmony with some vital principle that is above the law.'

There was almost a note of scorn in the Judge's voice as he framed the next question; 'And, because he said that, he thought that everybody else would believe it—is that what he told you?'

'I would not say that, my lord. The one thing he is not is a malingerer.'

'Does he appear to believe it?'

'Yes, absolutely.'

'He thinks he ought not to be punished?'

'Yes.'

'But does he really think he will not be punished? Does he think that if he is caught stealing or killing he will not be punished?'

'I asked him that and he said "I am awaiting the trial with complete equanimity; I am in the position of Jesus Christ before Pontius Pilate, and the only thing I have to say, if I was to say anything, it would be, 'He can have no power against me, unless it be given from above'." '

'That may well be,' Mr Justice Humphreys said, drily.

Giving evidence before the Royal Commission on Capital Punishment, Lord Goddard was asked about former New South Wales Minister of Justice, Ley, who was convicted in connection with the Chalk Pit murder, but reprieved. He made this astonishing admission: 'I thought he was insane from the way he gave his evidence'.

He was then asked, 'You would not think it proper that he should hang?'

He replied that he thought it perfectly proper. When the Lord Chief Justice of England can make a statement like this about a man he himself thought was insane, was it any wonder that another judge (only two years after the Chalk Pit case, incidentally) should have had so little regard for psychiatric evidence?

He testified that he had seen Haigh in Brixton Prison on five occasions between the 1st and 6th of July.

'What do you say is the mental state of the accused?' Sir David asked him.

'The first impression I gained of his mental state was that it was obvious that he had what is generally called a paranoid constitution. I had no doubt at all about that after my first interview with him.'

'Pausing for a moment at the paranoid constitution, what does that depend on and what are the formative features?'

'It is generally held to result from heredity and partly, or perhaps even more so, from environment, by which I mean specially the early upbringing, the home surroundings and early experience.'

Before Sir David could question Dr Yellowlees further on Haigh's home conditions and the religious background of those conditions, Judge Humphreys interjected, 'Before you go further, will you tell me what you are talking about? Are we going to have somebody from his home to prove the conditions under which he lived?'

'No, my lord,' said Sir David.

(I would submit that this was a cardinal error on the part of the defence.)

Mr Justice Humphreys then turned to Dr Yellowlees and asked, 'Then what are you telling me? Have you interviewed people at his home?'

'No,' said Dr Yellowlees. 'I said, "On the facts and statements shown to me on his history".'

'Do you mean what he says about himself, or what other people say about him?' was the Judge's next question.

'Both, my lord.'

'We cannot have what other people say about him,' the Judge ruled. 'That is second-hand evidence. You can tell us what he says about himself but we cannot have what somebody else is supposed to have said about him.'

When Dr Yellowlees was allowed to continue with his evidence, he said, 'He (Haigh) made it clear from what he said to me that he was brought up in a fanatical religious atmosphere and he told me that newspapers and radio were both forbidden in his parents' house, that friends and neighbours were excluded and that the wrath and vengeance of God was over his head for every trifling misdemeanour. . . .

Continuing after further examination by Sir David, the sole witness for the defence said, 'I think any household with that atmosphere is bound to be the reverse of stable. In this matter of heredity it is believed and said that that is the only thing which is really transmitted, namely, a mental instability; there is no obvious disease transmitted, it is the mental instability.'

'What is the effect of solitariness on dealing with the problems of life and what is its effect on the way the mind works?'

'If you have a youth with inherited nervous instability, brought up in a solitary atmosphere and with the fear that unseen and punishing powers are all around him, he tends to run away from them in the only way he can—namely, into a world, in the first place of fantasy and fairy tale; he will not face his difficulties fairly, and he becomes progressively less able to do so. At first, he thinks merely of some clever way round of avoiding punishment and if it develops further, and if there is no clever way round, he goes into himself, into a world of fantasy, and makes an imaginary solution for himself and comes to believe in it.'

'From the history which he has given you, do you find illustrations of the formative action in bringing about a paranoid constitution?'

'Yes?'

Sir David then asked Dr Yellowlees whether, apart from the question of home life, did he attach any importance to the change of surroundings which occurred to him between ten and sixteen, the change from Plymouth Brethren surroundings to those pervading Wakefield Cathedral? Did he attach any importance to that?

'Yes,' Dr Yellowlees agreed. 'Great importance. Here was this boy or youth in a system or form of worship and belief in which he himself did not believe and of which he was frightened, and then he is plunged into the opposite extreme and a form of worship where ritual and mysticism held a very much more prominent place. By entering into that atmosphere he avoids, as I was just saying, the conflict between the beliefs which he entertained in his early religion and his developing mind which in a normal person would reject it.'

At this point, Mr Justice Travers Humphreys again saw fit to interpose:

'Do you mind if I ask you a question here because I do not know what this is all about? Did he tell you that he used to be a member of the Plymouth Brethren when he was quite young, and then joined, in some form or another, Wakefield Cathedral?'

'No, my lord. The only thing he said to me was, "I never believed in it"—referring to his early religious teaching.'

Judge, counsel and witness then indulged in some verbal ping-pong about Wakefield Cathedral before Sir David got around to asking about Haigh's apparent lack of sex life.

'Yes,' said Dr Yellowlees, 'there is a complete absence of any sexual activity or interest, and that, in itself, is of course an abnormal thing.'

'This is not a case where you are depending on the sort of Viennese psychology, that everything is related to sex?'

'No, it has nothing to do with that.'

Sir David then asked what importance the witness attached to the prisoner's apparent lack of sex life.

'It is an indication of some very great abnormality of some kind, that a physically healthy young man, who does not seem to be at all scrupulous in what he does, should have no interest in sex and sexual activity. It happens also to be stated in authoritative works that that is a thing you find in a paranoic, who sublimates his sexual energies into this worship of himself and his mystic fantasy.'

Dr Yellowlees was then questioned about Haigh's earlier convictions:

'He says that he has to live like anybody else, having good enough wits and rather better than his neighbours, he has to do the best he can, and he really does it to get the artist's joy in doing a good job; he says that he is like an artist painting a picture, when he has successfully diddled or hoodwinked his fellow creatures. That, of course, is typical of the early paranoid constitution, and shows the conceit and fantasy of it, just as you see in the petty trickster.'

There comes a time in nearly every important criminal trial when an experienced observer can forecast with a reasonable degree of accuracy what the verdict of the jury is going to be. It came in the trial of John George Haigh when Sir Hartley Shawcross, the Attorney General, got up to cross-examine Dr Yellowlees:

'You said when you gave your evidence that you had seen the prisoner five times, you had examined him five times? That is not accurate, is it?'

Dr Yellowlees: 'I believe it to be accurate or I should not have said so.'

'Look at your notes,' Sir Hartley suggested suavely. 'When did you see him first?'

'I really do not know the dates—between the 1st and 6th of July.'

'Would you accept it from me that the first time you saw the prisoner was on the first of July?'

'Yes.'

'For twenty-five minutes?'

'Yes, I dare say.'

'The second time on the 2nd of July for one hour?'

'Yes.'

'And the third time on the 5th of July for 45 minutes?'

'Yes.'

'You visited Brixton Prison on two other occasions and discussed the matter with Dr Matheson?'

'Yes.'

'You never saw the prisoner, did you?'

'I do not think that is quite right,' Dr Yellowlees answered. 'I am prepared to accept it, and I am sorry if I made a mistake.'

Sir Hartley almost purred his next observation and question, saying, 'I do not want you to accept anything which is not right. I want you merely to be accurate. Have you not any notes of your interviews?'

'I have got large notes of the interviews with the prisoner, but I have not got notes of the days on which I actually visited him.'

For an experienced expert witness this was an extraordinary admission on the part of Dr Yellowlees. Those of us in the cramped, crowded seats allocated to the press could scarcely believe our ears.

'I must put it to you that you saw him in all for two hours and ten minutes, forty minutes longer than your evidence has so far taken,' said Sir Hartley. 'Is that right?'

'I do not know,' said Dr Yellowlees.

'Is it about right?'

'I do not know.'

'Is it about right?' the Attorney General persisted.

'I have got no idea.'

Reporters' pencils and pens were racing over their notebooks as Shawcross tried to pin Yellowlees down, patiently, courteously but ruthlessly.

'Let us see if we can agree about this. You would agree, would you not, that the prisoner is a person on whose word it would be utterly unsafe to rely?'

'Yes.'

'But you have, as a matter of fact, relied on it entirely, have you not, as the main basis of your opinion in this case?'

'No.'

'Have you not?'

'No.'

'What objective signs of insanity are there in the prisoner?'

'I should have to repeat all my evidence to show that,' Dr Yellowlees protested.

'Far be it from me to ask you to do that,' Shawcross replied with a politeness that was frigid, if not scathing. 'What objective signs of insanity are there apart from what the prisoner has said to you?'

'There are no such things as objective signs of insanity,' Dr Yellowlees retorted, trying to recover his composure. 'It is one of the oldest fallacies.'

'Then you are relying, are you not, in the main upon what the prisoner said to you?'

'No,' said Dr Yellowlees, with some heat. 'I am relying on my lifelong knowledge of such cases, and my observation of a cumulative series of symptoms, as I said.'

'What symptoms are you referring to apart from what the prisoner said to you? Mention one.'

'I am relying upon his verbosity, his egocentricity, the fact that he is unable to speak the truth, the fact that he has no shadow of remorse or shame for his deeds, the stories which he tells me about his dreams, and the fact that paranoia is, I think, the most difficult of all mental disorders to simulate and I do not think—I may be wrong, but I do not think I would have been hoodwinked.'

This was perhaps Dr Yellowlees' most telling piece of evidence, but it did not suffice. It did not carry as much weight with the jury as the question Sir Hartley Shawcross put to him later, 'Did you ever ask the prisoner how much he had realised in pounds, shillings and pence from the murders of the Hendersons and the McSwans to which he confessed?'

Dr Yellowlees replied that he did not consider it his province.

'The financial results of the offences he committed, you believe are wholly irrelevant?'

'Medically speaking, I think, yes.'

The Attorney General delivered his *coup de grâce* when he asked Yellowlees, 'I am asking you to look at the facts and tell the jury whether there is any doubt that he must have known that according to English law he was preparing to do and subsequently had done something which was wrong?'

'I will say "yes" to that if you say "punishable by law" instead of "wrong".'

'Punishable by law and, therefore, wrong by the law of this country?'

'Yes, I think he knew that.'

Sir Hartley Shawcross sat down. He had set the trap and Dr Yellowlees had fallen into it.

Thirteen years after the Haigh trial, the pathologist in the case, Professor Keith Simpson wrote a book called *A Doctor's Guide to Court, a Handbook on Medical Evidence* (Butterworth, 1962) in which these words of wisdom occur:

> There must be a limit of reason—and of honesty—to the views of a doctor might be prepared to state in evidence; there usually is, and seldom indeed does one now see acrimonious contests between experts that at one time did so much to discredit them in the eyes of the public, and of both law and medicine.

In this medical *vade-mecum*, Professor Simpson writes:

> Doctors must be prepared for a rather cold appraisal of their gifts and long experience from 'the other side'.

On the same theme, he continues:

> Finally, patience: the longer the doctor adheres quietly to the words he has carefully chosen and refuses to accept substitute words that counsel would like to use in their place—so long as it can be shown that the evidence supports the use of the original phrasing—the more likely it becomes that counsel will drop the point and pursue another line, or perhaps give up altogether. Objection should be made at once if, as occasionally happens, counsel deliberately misquote a reply or re-phrase it as a 'so it comes to this' kind of comment that may slip by unnoticed. 'You are using a word that I did not use' or 'No, the words you now use give a different meaning to my reply', will be sufficient.

Professor Simpson, on another page, says:

> Almost the only field of open dispute among doctors in criminal courts is that of 'insanity' (under the McNaughton Rules) or 'diminished responsibility' (under the Homicide Act, 1957)—especially the former. The evidence required from psychiatrists by the law is not always understood by them; insanity-at-law is not just mental disease.

Haigh, of course, was found guilty by the jury by strict adherence to the McNaughton Rules, or possibly misapplication of those rules dating from 1843, those antiquated rules which Robert S. Smith, LL.B. referred to in *The Criminologist* in the following terms: 'It was perhaps due to that unhappy piece of legislature—the McNaughton Rules—that the English criminal law had for so many years to lag behind the Continental and Scottish legal systems in its approach to the insane offender.'

The trial Judge, Mr Justice Humphreys, went into meticulous detail in explaining the McNaughton Rules to the jury of eleven men and one woman in the Haigh case. In the course of his summing-up, he said:

'Poor Daniel McNaughton had the delusion which is known among doctors as the delusion of persecution and which is very common. He thought that a number of people had conspired against him and that they used to send people into his room at night and worry him and so forth, and one of the people he thought had so conspired was the Prime Minister of the day, Sir Robert Peel, and he made up his mind to come to London with a pistol and get rid of Sir Robert Peel because, he said, "he is in conspiracy to make my life impossible". He came to London, he went to Downing Street which is the official residence of the Prime Minister, and there he shot the first person who came out of the front door, he standing in the street. In point of fact, it was not Sir Robert Peel, it happened to be Sir Robert Peel's secretary, a Mr Drummond, who was shot and killed. It makes no difference whatever in law that it happened not to be Sir Robert Peel but Mr Drummond who was killed; the man is *prima facie* guilty of murder.

'He was tried, and he was tried by Chief Justice Tindal, who directed the jury, and that direction which was given to the jury by that Chief Justice was afterwards approved by all the judges who met in solemn conclave, which I will mention to you in a moment. All of them agreed that Chief Justice Tindal was right according to the law of the land then, not according to the judges who made up the law at all but that it was and always had been—I will not say "always had been"—but had been for a long time—the law of the country.

'I am going to read to you just what Chief Justice Tindal said on that occasion, because it is very relevant to the issue which you have to try in this case. He said "The question is whether this man had the competent use of his understanding so that he knew he was doing a wicked and wrongful thing. If he was not sensible that it was a violation of the law of God or man, undoubtedly he was not responsible for the act or liable to any punishment whatever." That is exactly what he told the jury. Does it not read to you almost, not precisely in the same words, but almost exactly the law which counsel on both sides have told you, is the law today? It is the same thing. Had he competent understanding so as to enable him to appreciate that what he was doing was wrong?'

The wise old Judge then went on to refer to the fact that the defence had not put a single question to any of the witnesses for the prosecution relative to the prisoner's state of mind.

'What has been done here is that one witness has been called. The man himself might have given evidence if he had wished; he being sane now, as everybody agrees, he could have been called to tell us what he thought he was entitled to do or anything of that sort. I am not suggesting for a moment that he ought to have been called, but all I am saying is he is an admissible witness who could have been called. His father might have been called to say that the upbringing of this boy was very strict and he suddenly became a very High Churchman, he went as a chorister to a very High Church and that seemed to turn his head, if those are the facts—"We noticed at home this, that and the other." This is a very common form of evidence. But no, they are content to say to you: "We call an expert, an expert upon insanity and the diseases of the mind, who has formed an opinion."

'Members of the jury, if I were to say to you that you ought to follow the opinion of Dr Yellowlees, that would be in terms telling you to find a verdict of guilty in this case, because there is no doubt that Dr Yellowlees, although it was very much against his will, was in the end forced to say: "I cannot doubt that this man did know what he was doing"—he said so in terms—"and that it was wrong; I cannot doubt that".'

In point of fact, Dr Yellowlees did not say exactly that, and the learned Judge was wrong in implying that he did so, although the equally learned doctor had allowed himself, under Sir Hartley's cross-examination to accept an interpretation of Haigh's state of mind which was the opinion of the Attorney General and not his own. In other words, to use a commonplace expression, he had allowed the Attorney General to 'put words into his mouth'.

Between them, Mr Justice Humphreys and Sir Hartley Shawcross succeeded in blowing the case for the defence inside out, just as effectively as the gales of the previous Sunday had blown innumerable umbrellas inside out.

In his final words to the Sussex jury 'to which this man was entitled', the Judge said, 'It has not been put to you by Sir David Maxwell Fyfe that because a man commits two or three murders he is necessarily insane or that there is the slightest indication that he is insane. If any of you had the slightest idea that you could possibly draw such an inference, I would remind you of a case tried not so very many years ago in which a man was actually convicted of three separate murders, three wives, and which was known as the case of Smith and the "Brides in the Bath"; a man who was proved to have married a woman, murdered her, married another, murdered her, married another and murdered her; and nobody suggested he was insane.'

To me it is astounding that this part of the Judge's summing-up was allowed to go unchallenged. George Joseph Smith was *not* convicted of three separate murders because it is an axiom of English law that no man—or woman—can be charged with more than one murder at one and the same time. Smith was charged and convicted of but one murder—although evidence was permitted regarding the other two.

Scrutinising Mr Justice Humphreys' charge to the jury, one cannot help being aware of occasional slipshod phraseology, statements that are not entirely accurate. For instance, he referred to the 'Brides in the Bath' case as having taken place 'not so many years ago'.

George Joseph Smith was hanged in 1915. John George Haigh was hanged in 1949. Thus, no less than thirty-four years had elapsed between the trial of Smith and the trial of Haigh. But to an octogenarian thirty-four years may seem 'not so many years ago', although it was considerably more than a third of Sir Travers Humphreys' own life-span.

It would appear that the members of the jury had made up their minds before they were directed to retire, because the foreman asked, 'My lord, it is the jury's desire—would you allow us to retire?'

The jury retired at 4.23 p.m. and returned in less than twenty minutes with a unanimous verdict of 'Guilty'.

Asked whether he had anything to say why sentence of death should not be passed upon him according to law, Haigh said, 'Nothing at all.'

As the Judge was leaving the Court, an old woman broke through the police cordon and ran towards his stately limousine.

'Thank God for British justice,' she shouted.

The Condemned Cell

It was with some degree of distaste that John George Haigh had to change from his beloved Lovat green suit, foulard tie and shiny shoes into the officially approved clothing of a man condemned to death, a sack-cloth-like suit with tabs instead of buttons, white socks instead of his Mum's hand-knitted ones and slippers instead of his brogues. Then, with a 'death watch screw' on each side of him, as attentive as hotel porters showing a prized resident to his room, he was taken to the condemned cell.

He had no complaints about the verdict and wrote to tell his parents that he considered the Judge's summing-up as 'a classic'. There was still a chance that the Home Secretary might grant a reprieve and send him to Broadmoor, but Haigh entertained no false optimism about that. On the eighth day of the eighth month, two days before his execution he wrote:

Dearest Mum & Dad,

I have now had officially delivered to me the decision of the home secretary which I think you will have gathered from previous letters I was quite anticipating.

There have actually been too many fours in this affair for it to be otherwise. This is my fourth conviction, it's my fortieth year, the shopping list mentioned as one of the exhibits was No. 4 on the list. I was roughly on remand for four months. There were four remands and now there will be 22 (4) days from the 18th July to the 10th August. So that one can hardly say, I think that Ecclesiastes was wrong when he wrote what is, is & what shall be, shall be. When Somerfield eventually writes his book he'd better call it 'England Awake'. For she is still asleep to the fact that she executes her heretics. One day she may become enlightened. Too, the portents whilst I remember them: I had a short dream at Brixton. I was with you. Mother was doing some needlework, Father standing by the fire-place was saying 'Of course, he'll hang; they won't understand.' Then there was your own dream of my going up the steps.

I shall write you again. Don't be downcast,

Sonnie.

Several days previously, he had written:

Many thanks for yours.... It is very interesting to hear that you have heard from Australia; I am not really surprised as the Australian press was represented at Horsham & Lewes. I have not however had one myself although you appear to have been informed that a letter is on the way. I hope I get it. I had a very nice letter from Albert Ferber this week. He would still like to be able to play to me. The home office sent word through last night that Somerfield can come to see me for which I am very glad as he will be able to come along to you which though it may not be perfectly satisfactory to you as seeing me yourself it will give you a certain satisfaction I'm sure. I had a panel of men* to see me the day before yesterday. They wanted to know what I thought of the verdict. Of course I have already told you that it was a classic summing up and according to law within this country no other verdict could be arrived at. But other nations are more enlightened than we are. They don't hang people for their religious convictions even though Sacrifice is involved in the religious rite. We on the other hand

* From the Home Office.

have got passed (*sic*) the days of beheading heretics. This case *may* be a wonderful day for England. It may make them realise that religious freedom is not yet complete. If so, I shall go down in history as another martyr to my faith as great as Cranmer or any other.

Lots of love, Sonnie.

In the light of this letter alone, can it be claimed that John George Haigh was sane? At this stage he knew his fate, pehaps was looking forward to it. There was no point in feigning madness in a letter to his parents.

On the 29th of July, less than two weeks before his execution, he had written:

Dearest Mum & Dad,

... You must I suppose be so concerned about causing you that worry in face of my disregard of it in connection with the case as a whole. But that you see is something which I might avoid. Whereas these sacrifices—a word which intrigued Dr Snell of Wormwood Scrubs could not be avoided. To use your own phraseology God moves in a mysterious way. So that being led by an undeniable urge I was not given to discover what discomfort this might cause to myself or others. Spiritual conviction does not take into account the opinions or feelings of opposed thought. When the great spirit of Infinity constrained Israel to go out and slay each man his brother he did not take into account the injunction of Moses: thou shalt not kill. It may have been contrary to the moral laws of this land but then moral laws are merely relative. It is not so in every country in the world. The spiritual conviction of the individual is above mere (unenlightened) man made law. When one is convinced of propulsion by higher power one disregards man. One does not even think about it.*

Thank you for the YEN (Yorkshire Evening News) cutting,

* Author's Note: This confirms what Dr Noël Browne told me when I first consulted him regarding my attempt to 'walk through the mind of John George Haigh'. 'A man like Haigh does not stop to consider what is right or wrong when he commits his crimes,' he said.

[Haigh continues in his letter]. I found it very intriguing, particularly regarding the ages, which they got somewhat mixed, and the tall, upright husband. If they describe Dad as tall then what can I be? A lamp post?

I'm glad the Sunday version gave you pleasure although being ignorant of it I can't of course pass judgment. I do agree that this business of not being allowed newspapers is a very outmoded convention. I am also pleased to learn that you received solace from so many unknown sources. The judgment of the court was indeed a proper one, the prerogative of the court being one of justice according to law. The prerogative of the Home Secretary is of course not one of justice according to law, but justice according to mercy which involves consideration of more than mere patent facts: it involves consideration of moral principle and conviction of the individual.

I quite appreciate your decision not to make the journey which I do think which would be beyond your present powers of endurance, and hope that the Home Office will permit Somerfield to visit me in your stead. He has been so very kind and considerate in visiting you so many times and attending to your needs. Of course, the visit of the other gent I regard in the light of the old Greek proverb: 'Beware the lips that drip with honey', and therefore do not wholly share your views. May you find comfort in your own spiritual resources.

All my love, Sonnie.

None of the letters written by Haigh's parents to him when he was in the death cell appear to have survived. Perhaps Haigh himself destroyed them or possibly they gather dust in some Home Office archive, but I do have a copy of a letter to the condemned man, from a cousin, which expressed anguish similar to that which the aged parents must have experienced.

The writer was Fred Harris of Beechwood Avenue, Wakefield:

Dear John George, [he wrote] I feel it my duty to write to you, but how difficult it is, please understand George, I want you to know how deeply I feel about you and that I pray for you night and day, with all my heart and soul, for you are my Cousin after all. Please have faith in God even in this terrible hour, for in Him you still have hope, Remember the Thief on the Cross, George. I was the black sheep of my family and I am still far from Christ but I know I carn't (*sic*) go on forever like it. All the same I know the Power of prayer, thank God, so don't lose faith George. Be strong he alone can save you, and to that end I Pray. And I know I shall not Pray in vain. God bless you, Cousin Fred.

It is possible at this stage to quote only snippets from Haigh's letters to his parents while awaiting trial for the murder of Mrs Durand-Deacon. I select them because, in my opinion, they give some clues to the apparent complexity of his character.

In the spring, he wrote, 'Everybody seems to complain about the shortage of cuckoos this year. Have you noticed it too? Apparently there are not so many about as they usually are.'

Again, on the same theme, 'I think all the cuckoos must have come north because there have been screeds in the papers their absence hereabouts.'

Conscious of his love of music, his parents had asked, somewhat naïvely, if they could send a gramophone into him.

On the 8th of July, ten days before his trial, he replied: 'No; no gramophone—please! I might swallow the needles!'

He reveals that he is a great admirer of Sir Winston Churchill, but loathes Sir Stafford Cripps—'the old acid drop.' He says that if Churchill had not been in the Government he might have been in Parkhurst.

On the 30th of May, he wrote from Brixton, 'Dear Mum & Dad, What do you think of old Churchill's snort at the weekend. A magnificent oration, eh?

'I was very amused at the knock he gave Cripps. . . . It is a fact that Cripps goes to the Roffey Institution* every few months

* The Roffey Hospital, Horsham, containing 109 beds for psychiatric patients.

for treatment. I remember matron saying they had to watch him otherwise he would have been wandering round the place in the nude. I tell you the country is run by a load of lunatics at the moment.'

In June he writes 'Dearest Mum and Dad, I've just finished a very interesting book about worms. Their ability to completely replace the top soil is nothing short of amazing and the speed at which they breed is like an example of geometric progression from Hair and Knight. There are people in America who breed them in culture beds to sell to farmers for refurbishing their land. Apparently from a hundred worms it is possible to breed five million in two years!'

He is grateful for the flowers that have been sent to him. On the the 8th of June he writes, 'The pinks stand primly peeping over the top of my water jug. They are very pretty. The garden must be very fine just now. Is this the time when all that white stuff should be out?'

A month previously he had written, 'Dearest Mum & Dad, Thank goodness I'm not a Communist. We had a barage (*sic*) of singing (Red Flag) outside here yesterday. As bad as the Jews around the Wailing Wall. . . .'

Haigh, unlike most prisoners, did not look forward to visitors from the outside world. Some visits irritated him. Of a friend named George, he wrote, 'He was extolling your virtues. But sentiment is a thing which irritates me, and he is given to a precipitation into a very sloppy sentimentality which makes visits unbearable.'

In June he writes to his parents about a feature in *Picture Post* on Royal Ascot: 'Ascot is not so gay as it was in Teddie's day, or Victoria's. But life generally was much more worth while in those days. Can you imagine Teddie charging up Park Lane in tails and topper on a handsome (*sic*) from which he had deposed the cabbie at 5 o'clock in the morning these days?'

His enthusiasm for the Edwardian era, about which he could have known very little, carries him away: 'The police have got no sense of humour; he'd (Edward) have been locked up. But in those days they looked upon it as part of the fun of life. They even lock people up for climbing trees. Whereas then they looked on and cheered. Life is much too drab nowadays. No one possesses the capacity for enjoying simple pleasures. They are much too drab: too wrapped up in forms and encompassed by government restrictions. It's time there was a revolution!'

He congratulates his parents on their garden: 'Glad to hear your London Pride is doing so well—green fingers!'

Again, he writes, 'I suppose the garden looks green now after the rain, last night. I have no doubt it will please the farmers.'

In the condemned cell, he puts his parents off coming to see him, thus: 'I did warn you that it would be much better for you if you did wish to come to do so before the trial. I was then in my own clothes and there would have been much more freedom. As it is now I will warn you so that you shan't be disappointed that you will visit me in prison clothes among the coy. of two warders with no facility for "familiarisation".'

To console his parents, nine days before his execution, he writes with undoubted sincerity and a belated show of genuine affection, 'Be not downcast that things do not always remain as they are. If I remember rightly Ecclesiastics was one of your old favourite sources of inspiration. Now what does he say? "Say not how, what is the cause that the former days were better than these? For thou dost not inquire wisely concerning this". It is better to go to the house of mourning than the house of feasting for sorrow maketh glad the countenance.'

Perhaps Haigh was writing his own epitaph. On the morning that he met the hangman there was no sorrow on his countenance, only gladness.

'They could not save your son'

On the sunlit morning of August 10, 1949, two men had the melancholy task of writing to Haigh's parents. One was Mr Stafford Somerfield, journalist, the other Mr J. Ireland Eager, solicitor of Horsham, Sussex. Mr Somerfield wrote in great sorrow 'to tell you that despite all the efforts that were made they could not save your son . . . his bearing in the end was magnificent. He showed the greatest possible courage and, I believe, was completely composed . . . His last thoughts were of you both and were expressed with great kindness and dignity.

'I believe, as you know I do, that the world did not see the real side of your son. This side you knew, and of which I was permitted to catch a glimpse, was one of great charm and natural affection. The other side can only have been placed there by some evil force of which we are only dimly aware, and cannot understand.'

Mr J. Ireland Eager's letter was much more business-like. 'My retainer to act on his (Haigh's) behalf was determined by his Execution and as the files and papers may have some bearing on his estate, if any, I have been advised by Counsel to forward them to you for safe custody.'

This echoes Haigh's own words when he wrote to his parents: 'Nobody will ever understand me.'

It would be as well to try to catch a glimpse of the better side of Haigh. Let us look at Haigh as seen through the eyes of some people who knew him and were absolutely dumbfounded when they read of his arrest and the nature of his crimes.

Among them were Mrs Sophy Feuerheerd, her son Tom, and her daughters, Patricia and Rosemary—the girls whom Haigh had described only the previous Christmas as looking 'absolutely devastating', and the talk of the hotel. The Feuerheerds lived at 3 Roland Gardens, South Kensington, not far from the Onslow Court Hotel, and Haigh was a frequent visitor to their home, sometimes too frequent, although he was always made welcome. Whenever the bell rang, Mrs Feuerheerd would say, 'That must be John again.' He became almost one of the family.

John George Haigh was not only a friend of the family—he was a friend to the family. Mr Teddie Feuerheerd had been in the wine trade but in later years had become entirely absorbed in various inventions of his own. He was no crank inventor. Two of his inventions are in the South Kensington Science Museum, but he had little or no success in marketing his ideas.

Mr Feuerheerd happened to confide in a chemist, who had premises in the Old Brompton Road, something of his frustration. The chemist said he knew just the chap who might be able to help —a go-ahead young fellow who was a bit of an inventor himself. (The description was more accurate than the chemist quite realised!) An introduction was arranged, and Haigh met the Feuerheerd family.

From the outset Haigh was enthusiastic about Mr Feuerheerd's inventions. He said he would find the necessary capital to market them. He did, in fact, provide about £1,000 altogether, although he had no success in marketing the ideas. Where he found the capital can only be a matter for speculation, but the Feuerheerds had no reason to suppose that he was not what he purported to be, a successful man of business.

He was popular with the entire family, father, mother, son and two daughters. He was kindness itself, sometimes to the point of embarrassment. 'I remember my mother complaining how difficult it was to get Ovaltine during those days of rationing,' Patricia, now Mrs R. L. Troop, told me. 'John Haigh was present and on his very next visit arrived with a seven pound tin of cocoa. It was embarrassing but we felt that John meant well, that he always meant well.'

The family did not realise that this outsize tin of cocoa might have come from the kitchen or the store-room of the Onslow Court Hotel.

The Feuerheerds gave frequent dinner parties and John Haigh became a regular guest. The parties were informal, happy affairs where the conversation quite often turned to music, the ballet and the arts. (Rosalind Feuerheerd, now married and living in California, joined the Covent Garden Ballet.) There is no doubt that Haigh thoroughly enjoyed these *soirées*, meeting people he would not otherwise have met, relishing perhaps for the first time a warm and lively family atmosphere that must have been a refreshing change from the arid one of an hotel dining room, and a delightful contrast to the drab life he had known as a boy in the little house in Ledger Lane.

Albert Ferber, the concert pianist, was also a guest, and Haigh often took Mrs Feuerheerd and sometimes her daughters, to Ferber's recitals.

There is no doubt that Haigh liked to be seen around with good-looking girls, the younger the better. Rosalind and Patricia Feuerheerd were some twenty years his junior.) All the evidence is that he never even attempted mild petting. He was a perfect little gentleman.

When the news of Haigh's arrest was headlined and his photograph smiled from the front pages, Albert Ferber could not believe his eyes. He telephoned Patricia and said, 'Can this really be the same man?'

The Feuerheerds, shocked beyond belief, were asking themselves the same question, as no doubt were many others. The Feuerheerds were to receive confirmation that was too close for comfort. Detectives arrived on their doorstep.

Just over a year previously, Mr Feuerheerd had died. John

George Haigh had attended the funeral at Golders Green Crematorium. After the service, he said that he wished he could have played the organ for his friend. The widow had been quite touched by this sentiment. She was equally touched by Haigh's generosity. He offered to pay her rent—and did.

The detectives who called at 3 Roland Gardens were inclined to be cynical about Haigh in the role of a benefactor. They were perhaps under the impression that Mr Feuerheerd's death was another one 'down to chummie', a murder to which Haigh had *not* confessed, but it was indisputably established that the inventor had died from natural causes.

To this day Mrs Feuerheerd refuses to believe that John George Haigh ever thought of her husband, herself or her children as possible victims. She does not believe that Haigh could have contemplated wiping out her family as he wiped out the McSwans.

'I had known only the good side of him,' she told me. 'No matter how terrible his crimes, I could not in all conscience forget that he had been good to me and a welcome guest in my home.'

When Mrs Feuerheerd had recovered sufficiently from the shock, she wrote to Haigh—and to his mother. Neither letter could have been easy to write, but both were deeply appreciated and she kept up the correspondence with Haigh until the end, and with Mrs Haigh after the execution.

'My dear Sophie,' Haigh replied from Brixton Prison, misspelling her name. 'Very many thanks for your kindly and understanding letter: also for the lovely letter which my mother informs me you have sent to her. I hope she is going to meet you. She knows how kind you have been to me and that I dearly love you all.

'I face the future with complacency fearing not what man can do; for he still gropes in the darkness and comprehends not the light; not having learned to drink of the water of life, saying platitudinously that blood is thicker than water and knowing not what it means.

'But there is no good in my exposing that thought as nobody ever understands me.

'Tom will doubtless have told you that I have arranged for patent renewal fees and all matters thereto to be cared for so long as I am unable to do so personally. Also the Walpole Investment Trust.

'It is with joy that I remember those heavens that I have known in the many happy days I have spent with you the most wonderful family that any man could be privileged to know.

'My love to you all,

John.'

Accept Haigh as a monster. Accept him as a glib and unscrupulous liar, but I do not believe that there was anything glib about this letter. I am sure he remembered with joy the happy times he had spent with the inventor, his wife and children. And when he describes them as the most wonderful family any man could have been privileged to know, there can be no doubting his sincerity. Herein is a clue to the terrible secret he managed to conceal behind his smiling blue eyes. At 3 Roland Gardens he found peace of mind, basked in the warmth of being liked, and enjoyed glimpses of a home life that he had never known as a youth.

Haigh's genuine affection for the family is more than confirmed by his mother who wrote:

'Dear Mrs Feuerheerd, I do appreciate your sympathy and kindly remarks regarding our dear son. Also I thank you for your invite to come and see you if I come to London.

'My visit will mostly depend on John's wishes. I have asked him to let me know if he would like to see me. What a tragedy! What a tragedy!

'At home he has always been most lovable and affectionate. He was very touched at the passing of your dear husband and often spoke of the very happy times he spent with you all.

'May God have mercy and comfort his dear soul in isolation,

'Yours very sincerely, Emily Haigh.

'P.S. Many thanks for all the pleasures you have given to our dear boy. My heart is too sad for his sake.'

Something of the agony endured by Mrs Haigh is indicated by a subsequent letter to Mrs Feuerheerd. On the 8th of March, she writes:

'My dear Friend, Thank you so much for your letter and the kindly offer to come and see me. I was much encouraged by the expression—"but somehow one manages to carry on".

'I'm thankful that it is so. So far, I am still awaiting my son's sanction to say when I can go to see him. At first his counsellor thought it unadvisable for me to visit him but I should love to see him.

'John told us he had received another nice letter from you. Please accept my heartfelt thanks for the pleasure and comfort you render him in this dark hour in which he is beset.

'The tragedy is incomprehensible and to think what the end of it shall be. Well, overwhelming I'm afraid. He writes home cheerfully on the whole. His solicitor is extremely thoughtful and kind by informing us how he is from time to time. . . .

'Again thanking you for your love and sympathy,

Yours sincerely, Emily Haigh.'

It is quite obvious that Mr and Mrs Haigh suffered far more acutely than their son, who was unmoved by his fate and awaiting the end with—to use his own word—complacency.

'Dear Mrs Feuerheerd,' his aged mother writes on July 21st, 1949. 'I thank you for all the kind and certainly comforting letters you have sent to me.

'I should also like to thank you and others of your family for writing to John so often. I know he did appreciate that. It often gladdened my heart to know that he had friends who cared for him. But now what will he do!

'No daily papers to read. No one to converse with, and nothing we can do to mitigate the monotony.

'It's an overwhelming grief and we know what shall be the end of it. The verdict on Tuesday was the supreme penalty. I wonder if there will be an appeal.

'I'm thankful to say that my husband and I have held up well so far but the strain is beginning to show signs of overcoming our endurance for our mellowing years.

'I hope you and all your family are well. I know you will miss John's company as he does yours. He has told me what happy evenings he has spent with you and friends. To write this makes my heart sick and sad. Again thanking you all for the pleasures you have given him.

'Yours grateful and sincerely, Emily Haigh.'

The correspondence did not end with the execution of Haigh. On July 28th, 1950, four days after what would have been his forty-first birthday, the grief-stricken mother wrote:

'Dear Mrs Feuerheerd, Thank you so much for your welcome message received this wk.

'I was not anticipating such a sweet reminder of the 24th. So that it deeply touched me, and I realised that John still holds a place in your heart's affection.

'I remember how kindly he always spoke of your family, and your dear husband he admired him. I do find it difficult to understand the mystery of John's life. It was never himself: he was always so gentle and loveable at home.

'So whatever could it be unless "What has to be will be", if not, then the "predilection of the Almighty".

'Some days my heart feels torn to pieces as well as my nerves, as you notice how unsteady my hand is.

'It's terrible when I think of his last moments on earth and know he will never come home again.

'My husband and I find more peace of mind in living an insulate life. Friends would like to visit us but I don't receive any. All our interest has gone concerning this world. . . .

'Yours affectionately, Emily Haigh.'

Another year goes by and again Mrs Feuerheerd remembers to send Mrs Haigh a letter of solace on the occasion of her son's birthday, which the immeasurably unhappy mother acknowledges thus:

'Thank you for your loving and touching letter which I received this wk. May I tell you for a few days I wondered if I should receive a message from you for this occasion. It certainly did bring comfort and cheer to my still sore heart. It was also a reminder of the sincere friendship that existed between your family and John. Your husband was an ideal man to him. We have felt the loss of John's visit this wk. and we also miss the lovely letters he used to send regular & often. It is true we had the last and he won't come home any more. God only knows how mysterious his passing is to us and the change it has made in our life. I am thankful I have the letters he sent during his duress. I often read them, & as you say we can recapture the sound of voices and sayings of absent ones and picture them in the places they used to occupy.

'The real things are gone and we are left behind to bear a burden of sorrow and loneliness. It was John's wish that we should not grieve unduly. My husband and I are keeping tolerably well. In silence and solitude we choose to live the rest of our eventide days. My husband resents company as much as ever.

'We have been obliged to call in a Dr. It is the first time to happen to me. My nerves are bad and it is with difficulty to command my pen always. It's heart trouble with John (her husband). So there we are, still much to be thankful for. . . .

'I very much regret I am unable to make a definite arrangement for Rosemary to come to see us when she comes to Leeds. I would love to see her for John's sake. In his last letter to us August 9th (the day before his execution) he said he had received such a sweet letter from her that a.m. Dear Sonnie, his home pet name. I think the strain must have been too great for any of us to understand when he read his last letters. Yet when Mr Sommerville visited him the same afternoon he said John was wonderfully composed. I must close the subject. It becomes too vivid before my eyes. . . .'

I cannot believe that even the most rabid of those who bay

for the return of the rope can deny that the sentence of death carried out on John George Haigh served no useful purpose. He was impervious to his fate. The full might and majesty of the Law succeeded in inflicting dreadful punishment on his old parents, not on him. They suffered not only more than their son but, in a different way, more than his victims. The biblical precept of the sins of the father being visited upon the son was reversed.

On January 18th, 1955, Mrs Feuerheerd received a letter. 'I have to inform you with regret and at her special request, of the death of Mrs Emily Haigh in a Harrogate nursing home on January 5th.

Mrs Haigh talked about you only a day or two before her death and expressed her appreciation of the fact that you had kept in touch with her since the unhappy events of some years ago.

'The lady was confined to her bed for about three months and had a fair amount of bodily suffering before the end, which came as a merciful and—to her—welcome release.'

The signature was that of the executor to the Haighs' modest estate, the man to whom Mrs Haigh entrusted her son's letters to do with them as he felt fit, the man who was good enough to give me access to them.

We know that Mrs Haigh told him that she and her husband had despised their neighbours, thinking themselves the 'elect of God', and that she now knew how mistaken they had been.

Then she asked for a glass of water.

'Goodbye and God bless you,' she said. 'He will be my Pilot. He will pilot me through to the other side.'

'So it should be fun'

I do not think that even the late Sir Travers Humphreys or any other august judge could have sworn by Almighty God that a man who looked forward to his trial for murder as an occasion for fun could be considered even remotely sane. Yet such a man was John George Haigh.

It was on June 29th, 1949, less than three weeks before his trial, that Haigh wrote once again to Mrs Sophy Feuerheerd. It was a fairly long letter, filling almost all the available space on the buff writing paper supplied to the residents of HM Prison, Brixton, and it is typical of Haigh that the reference to his forthcoming trial is contained in the last brief paragraph, almost an afterthought or what actors call a throwaway line:

'Dear Sophie,

'Nice to hear from you again. Sorry to hear about Rosemary. Poor child she must have cut quite a pathetic figure. I heard from her yesterday and was on the point of replying which was a natural impulse born of Arthur's Round Table but it struck me that it might not be a good thing for her to receive one of these forms 243 under a strange roof—you never know who might get hold of it—(Haigh is referring to prison note-paper)—especially as I can't decipher the address with complete certainty and I wouldn't like to cause Rosemary embarrassment that way.

'So will you please thank her when you write & I'll drop her a line when she comes back. Tell her that I know Kirkcudbright having spent some very enjoyable holidays around Dalbretie, Castle-Douglas, Kipford (*sic*) etc. It should be very nice up there just now. Ask her if she has gone to the Velvet Path near Kipford also Mary's Tower on the other side of the Ur (*sic*) beyond Palnachie. Tell her that Port Talbot is a heavenly place for bathing. My kind regards to Maggie Reden.

'Ha Ha! I thought that was what might happen to Tom's bathroom. I can just imagine what it would be like. He may not be pleased with your erasions that's true, but at least it will be a pure wholesome colour which will give a proper hygenic atmosphere!

'I had Albert Ferber to see me yesterday. It was very nice indeed of him to take the trouble. I don't think there will be time left for him to get a concert fixed in however.

'Have you read Compton Mackenzie's *Hunting the Fairies*—you should it is riotously funny—in fact just your handwriting!

'Well there is only a fortnight just over to go to Lewes and there is quite a legal debate going on as to whether I can be tried at all! So it should be fun.

'Love John.'

So it should be fun! One cannot help pondering over this remark of a man about to go on trial for his life, looking forward to the occasion as if it were some jolly party. We know, as Dr Noël C. Browne has pointed out, that the written word can more easily be used to conceal a man's real feelings than the spoken word, but was this mere braggadocio on Haigh's part? I do not think so. Have we not his account of 'hooting with mirth' as he left Horsham magistrate's court in the police car?

Albert Ferber has told me of the visit he paid to Haigh in Brixton Prison. Haigh was completely unconcerned about his forthcoming trial, his attitude being that the whole thing was 'a misunderstanding'. Many a concert pianist has been more nervous before a recital than Haigh was before his public appearance at Lewes.

'He really was most knowledgeable, not only about music, but about musical instruments as well,' the pianist told me. 'We spent almost the entire half-hour, which was the duration of my visit, discussing old musical instruments, and he was remarkably well versed in the subject and he was very technical. There was a prison officer present, who endeavoured to take a note of our conversation, but the poor fellow had to give up eventually. It was quite beyond his comprehension.

'I can assure you that I had not been looking forward to the visit, but Haigh made me feel completely at ease. He appeared to be quite oblivious to the surroundings. We could have been in somebody's drawing-room.

'I came away more baffled than ever, again asking myself, "Can this be the same man who committed those terrible crimes?"'

Five days before he was due to be executed, Haigh wrote to Albert Ferber from the condemned cell at Wandsworth:

'Many thanks for your letter. . . . I can understand the artist in you straining at the leash as it were to come and give me spiritual uplift—as music is so much more to me than mere entertainment. I should dearly love to listen again to your inspired interpretations: but in the present position everything has to have the approval of the magistrates and time in that case is our enemy.

'Please accept my very deep gratitude for your persistent kindly solicitations. My every good wish goes with you until you achieve the pinnacle of success. It has been good to know you . . . and I hope you will derive satisfaction from the fact that your performances have provided me with many happy hours of reminscences.

'Yours sincerely, John.'

Haigh never loses an opportunity of referring to Albert Ferber in his letters to his parents, who did not know the pianist, and to the Feuerheerds, who did. He writes to Patricia in June:

'My dear Tricia,

'How very sweet of you. It is very nice to hear from you again. I often think of you all and in your particular case I seem always to remember the day we went to Kew at Magnolia time. 2 Last Christmas when you looked so distingue in the black lace shawl (You'll never believe the number of people who spoke about that later) 3 The Empress Hall concert of the little Italian boy although I can't remember his name. I think it was an experience not to be forgotten.

'I nevertheless think its good that my memory is bad in other directions. I don't remember at all my comments upon your card from Scotland. . . . May I belatedly wish you my many happy returns? I'm disappointed that I forgot it. I don't usually forget birthdays; but I believe you were always at school when the event occurred.

'I'm glad you had such a nice time; it must have been wonderful listening to Albert Ferber. I wish he could fulfil his own wish and play to me. A very nice thought of his: typically Russian—that is of the old Russian not of the present product. . . . I'm very glad to hear that he thinks so well of your playing; that is indeed a tribute.

'Thank you for the programme. I'm sure it was worth hearing. I saw the bleat in the Telegraph and was pleased to see that they are becoming sensible of his talent. I shall always remember the night when Teddie and I heard him at Wigmore. He was terrific. I was shocked by the critics. I don't think they had been there at all! . . .

'Am reading some very interesting books at the moment amongst which *World without Visa* by Jean Malaquais and *Granada Window* by Marguerite Steen are worth keeping your eyes open for.

'I wonder if you heard "Tommy"* make his marvellous speech at the A.H. It must have been a wonderful concert.

'Love to you all and many thanks for writing

'John.'

He writes to Patricia again on July 1st, again claiming to know Kircudbright well, again expressing enjoyment of Compton

* An obvious reference to Sir Thomas Beecham. Here again, Haigh adopts an attitude of familiarity.

Mackenzie's book, almost as if on holiday himself. The letter might have been written from a deck chair instead of a prison cell.

'It's nice to hear about what you are doing, you know. If this weather only persists you are bound to have a wonderful time in Cornwall. I can't reciprocate unfortunately as nothing exciting happens around these parts. The flag irises and the paeonies are over and there are now some geraniums and some anaemic looking yellow jobs decorating the garden....

'I've just finished reading a book which I think should cause you much amusement: *Hunting the Fairies*, Compton Mackenzie. About some American women tourists invading Scotland. One of them arrives with 41 Pekenese (*sic*). What pandemonica! I know the part of Scotland that Rosemary is in very well. Its a heavenly bit of country and if she has gone for a rest well she's not far from Kipford: the name itself is soporific. Thanks again for your news. With love

'John.'

Only three days before the commencement of his trial for the murder of Mrs Durand-Deacon, he again refers to the 'fun' possibilities.

'So Rosemary is going to America is she,' he writes to Mrs Feuerheerd. 'Good egg! Do you know it is the one country I have never had the slightest desire to visit. I think it would be just bedlam. They don't know how to settle down and enjoy life. Give me the peace of England's countryside even if we do have to pump water from the well and slide down icy paths in the winter to the outside whatnot. Well there should be some fun at Lewes next week. The excursions I am afraid are going to prove abortive. So let's hope the sun shines for the poor throng....

'Lots of love to all—John.'

He even manages to be light-hearted about his exercise in the prison yard, writing, 'Am having quite a busy time myself. Do about 4 miles a day—which means that since I came here I must almost be at Darlington.

'By the same token I should soon get to the Highlands in time for the grouse!'

Rarely is he at a loss for words. In only one letter does he confess that he is nonplussed. It is yet another letter to Mrs Feuerheerd, and he admits that he is bewildered. It is as if—briefly—his mask has slipped.

'When I think of you all, which is often,' he writes, 'I'm really very bewildered and am reminded of

"Not till the loom is silent and the shuttles cease to fly
"Shall God unfold the canvas and explain the reason why."
'Yours —?—

'Just what can I put there to express what I feel.
'John.'

This comes at the end of a letter that starts off cheerfully enough, saying that he hopes Rosemary will enjoy herself in Italy (where she was appearing with the Covent Garden Ballet) and he wonders whether she will meet Princess Margaret.

He appears to be far more concerned about the progress of Mr Feuerheerd's inventions than his own defence, reminding the inventor's widow that Mr Eager 'has sufficient funds at his disposal to look after any renewals and developments of any sort'. Also, is her rent due? If so, apply to Eager.

'Now is there anything else that you want me to help you with whilst the opportunity remains. Please don't hesitate to let me know. I do want to do everything I can to help you. . . .'

His use of the phrase 'whilst the opportunity remains' is significant. As he wrote to Albert Ferber in another letter, he knows that 'time is our enemy'.

It is a situation that offers a challenge to alienists, to psychiatrists, to all who call themselves criminologists. Here is a man who has horrified a nation that has only just emerged from a holocaust of horror. He is in prison, awaiting trial for the self-confessed murder of one widow in exceptionally brutal circumstances, disposing of her body in a way that made even case-hardened detectives blench. Ostensibly, he murdered this widow—and others—for profit.

Yet, in this prison cell, his chief concern appears to be for the financial problems of another widow. He tells his solicitor to pay her rent, to pay the patent fees on her late husband's inventions. He wants to help all he can. There can be no ulterior motive. Should the inventions prove a commercial success, he knows that he cannot benefit in any way.

His anxiety to help is quite disinterested. His letters to Mrs Feuerheerd are almost filial, even more so than those to his own mother. They are often touchingly tender. He writes almost as one of the family. How is Tom getting along? And Rosemary? And Tricia? He is sorry that Rosemary will miss Victor de Sabata's concert, but hopes she will enjoy herself in Italy: he jokes about the possibility of her meeting the Pope or Princess Margaret. He remembers how glamorous Patricia looked last Christmas in her black lace shawl. 'How is Trish getting along with the duets? Give her my love.' He even enquires after their dog, Cheeta.

Haigh's last letter to Mrs Feuerheerd from the condemned cell at Wandsworth was dignfied and moving.

'It is difficult to wish you farewell under these circumstances but I send you all my very sincere love and my greatest wish is that you shall continue successfully with your ventures. I need hardly tell you that the five years of association with your family provide me with the happiest memories of my life. As I have said: to know the Feuerheerds was like possessing an old world garden full of grace and charm. Success and the Almighty spirit's providence attend you. My love to each of you.

'Yrs John.'

In my view, the family at 3 Roland Gardens provided Haigh with a substitute family life—the sort of family life he had never known but desperately needed. That was why he was grateful and once at a loss for words. Perhaps if he *had* enjoyed that sort of family atmosphere earlier in his life his story would have been happily different and I would not have written this book.

There is no doubt that Haigh had a plural personality. Is not the Haigh in the prison cell, anxious about the finances of the widow in Roland Gardens, trying to make amends for that other Haigh who so pitilessly destroyed the widow from the Onslow Court Hotel?

The trial of Haigh lasted precisely two days, one day of which was given up to formal evidence that was never in dispute, much of which could well have been dispensed with. Surely, in a case where the only legal disputation was the question of Haigh's sanity, the medical evidence alone should have taken at least two days rather than two hours? One came away from the trial feeling that it had been conducted with almost indecent haste.

The trial of John George Haigh succeeded only in displaying the bankruptcy of some aspects of English law, the Justice which we never tire of proclaiming to be the envy of the world.

Haigh always maintained that monetary gain was not the only motive for his murders.

'There are so many other ways of making easy money even though illigitimately (*sic*), he wrote. 'It would have been much simpler to have got rid of my parents and inherited the property. There need have been no questions about that.'

This statement seems to indicate that at one time he must have contemplated murdering his parents, even when writing them affectionate letters. It is not surprising that the one phrase he used frequently was 'Nobody will ever understand me'. The fact is that he never understood himself and he revealed it when he wrote, 'I'm really very bewildered'!

That was his subconscious *cri-de-cœur*.

Psychiatric analysis by Dr Noël C. Browne

It is about time that criminality was accepted and treated as the product of emotional dysfunction that it is. It is also about time that the medical profession stopped being bullied by the legal profession while trying to indulge in psychiatric baby-talk about the infinitely complex process of human motivation, attitudes and actions, under stress or otherwise, in order to fit into the simplistic and archaic terms of the long out-of-date and never justified so-called McNaughton rules. McNaughton, how many judicial murders have been committed in thy name!

It is not simply sterile speculation to examine the process by which John George Haigh was executed for murdering six, and possibly nine, men and women, although of course only charged with one murder. In time he will join those unfortunates executed for sheep-stealing or picking pockets in another age, according to the then sacrosanct rules and laws of society.

The judicial process against Haigh proceeded with a fascinating precision and adhesion to correct protocol at all stages. Yet he could not have been hanged without the authority—help implies a supporting role—of the two great professions, the law and medicine, and in particular, the psychiatric branch of medicine. It is not remarkable that, in spite of society's centuries of experience of the pompous, fallible asininity of both these distinguished groups, they both still retain their authority? If the law is an ass, then psychiatry is simply a jackass.

In the context of our present belief about the wrongness of taking life, surely the case of J.G.H. must become another bloodied milestone in man's slow march from barbarism towards civilisation. Because J.G.H. could not have been hanged judicially murdered or simply executed without the support of the law and medicine, they gave the hangman his authority for doing his terrible act. The law looked for his life, and relied on the rigid demands of the out-moded 19th century McNaughton rules: and the psychiatrist had to accept the absurd black and white limitations imposed on him by these rules, in spite of their grotesquely simplistic limitations. It is conceivable that in 1843, when they were first applied, the rules were reasonable and rational given the state of knowledge or ignorance of the psychodynamics of human activity. At the same time, in the light of the law's enlightened belief, even as stated by the then Lord Chancellor, Lord Erskine, in his three categories of insanity, it is difficult to know how the McNaughton rules could ever be accepted as practically applicable in cases of criminal homicide. Lord Erskine dealt most eloquently with the 'delusions', which are infinitely various and after extremely circumscribed, which mock the wisdom of the wisest in judicial trials, because such persons often reason with a subtlety that puts in the shade the ordinary conceptions of man', and his other kind of insanity where 'the conclusions are just and often profound, but the premises from which they reason when within the range of the malady are uniformly false'. At a time when such a subtle and sensitive assessment of the insane mind was postulated, it is difficult to understand why, then or since, the crudely simplistic black or white demands of the McNaughton rules were ever used by the law and medical profession to take men's lives in retribution for the crime of homicide.

At the trial of J.G.H. there was no doubt that Haigh had murdered Mrs Durand-Deacon, as well as probably five, possibly eight other persons. The psychiatric evidence of Haigh's insanity was the only hope of saving him from execution.

Here it is pertinent to refer to the method in which the process operated.

Under the McNaughton rules, a person must know the nature and quality of the act he has committed, and that what he is doing is both wrong and punishable by law. Dr Yellowlees, a psychiatrist of considerable distinction and experience, gave evidence for the defence. Unfortunately for Haigh, he made a number of admissions that were damaging.

In reply to the Attorney General, he conceded the first point under the McNaughton rules, 'he knew murder was punishable by law, and he was like any other practical man, anxious to avoid it'. Then, on the vital question—'did he know what he was doing was wrong?'—Dr Yellowlees was asked, 'You are not prepared to express an opinion on whether he knew what he was doing was wrong?' 'That is so: I do not think that any psychiatrist could answer that question unless he had lived with a paranoid for years.'

The defence appears to have collapsed around the psychiatrist's evidence. It is particularly fascinating to watch how the attacking scepticism of Sir Hartley Shawcross completely changed the whole manner of Dr Yellowlees. The Attorney General's devastating opening questions seriously underlined the reliability of the evidence of this distinguished scion of the medical profession. Dr Yellowlees, showing a lack of precision—strange in such a desperately serious situation for his patient—wasn't sure whether he had paid three or five visits to Haigh while in jail. He was wrong, however, and wrong on the wrong side, in so far as he had overestimated and not underestimated the number of his visits. Rapidly deflated he frequently showed signs of insecurity before the concise clarity of the Attorney General. Whereas in the evidence for the defence Dr Yellowlees expounded at length in a way which now seems to be vague garbled generalisations about insanity in the face of Sir Hartley Shawcross's frightening irreverence he rapidly became a miser in his use of words, and where of course the need arose to question the lawlords' right to pin him to their terms of reference, a simplistic interpretation of the Mc-

Naughton rules he failed to save Haigh. While Shawcross quite rapidly gained a complete ascendancy over Yellowlees, he was helped by Yellowlees's opening admission of his cursory attitude to his visits to Haigh.

Furthermore, Yellowlees appeared to be at odds with the man whom he advanced as the supreme authority on the condition from which he said Haigh suffered—paranoia. Dr Yellowlees claimed that after his first visit to Haigh, which it, appears, lasted only twenty-five minutes, he diagnosed this condition of paranoia —'I have no doubt at all about that, after my first visit to him, exactly as described by the distinguished Florentine psychiatrist, Professor Tanzi.' Yet under questioning he later admitted that Professor Tanzi used 'terminology of forty years ago—it has no application whatever to our present conception of disease or to this particular case.' Why was Tanzi used as the authority on the basis of whose beliefs Haigh's life or death was decided?

Presumably Dr Yellowlees advised Counsel about the general line establishing Haigh's insanity. The preoccupation with the textbook description of Professor Tanzi's definition of pure paranoia, and the lengthy and discursive dissertation on the paranoid constitution as a precondition of pure paranoia, appear to have allowed the case to drift away from a detailed examination of Haigh's life-style, which in itself was the best explanation of the emotionally disturbed child-adolescent-adult man he became.

It is painful indeed to have to question the whole process of defence which centred around the very narrow and, I believe, completely unanswerable question 'Did Haigh at the time he murdered Mrs Durand-Deacon know that he did something which was for him, Haigh, wrong to do?' There is a world of difference between this question and the question 'Did Haigh know that he was, in the eyes of the laws of England, acting contrary to those laws?' Even if he knew it was wrong for him, as well as wrong in law, it is still quite impossible to say with certainty that Haigh arrived at either or both these conclusions as a result of the cold rational process of reasoning expected by the Courts of Law.

It seems indeed to question the rationality of the reasoning process whereby the hangman was authorised by the elaborate, pompous and all-powerful judicial process of lawyers, psychiatrists, judge and jury and prisoner. There is so much which was said and indeed left unsaid between the time Haigh went with Mrs Lane to Chelsea Police station to report the fact that Mrs Durand-Deacon was missing. Recall for a moment Lord Chancellor Erskine's definition of insanity—'such persons often reason with a subtlety that puts in the shade the ordinary concepts of mankind'. If we acknowledge the well-known extraordinary phenomenon of the emotionally disturbed person who seeks to have himself charged and convicted of murder—the individual with some bizarre manifestation of a sado-masochistic kind who yearns for death, and well-publicised death at that—why did a man with the generally accepted good level of intelligence which Haigh was known to have, not simply 'skip the country', or at least leave the hotel, the neighbourhood and the scene of the crime? Even if we accept that he hoped to end up in Broadmoor as a homicidal lunatic, surely the prospect of such a penalty would be sufficiently powerful to persuade him to try to escape before the details of the murder were found out. Was Haigh a deeply guilt-ridden individual for whom the only possibility of peace was either that of execution and death, or did he contemplate life imprisonment? If the former were true, then it could be said that the whole elaborate and wonderful judicial process—which was after all set in motion by Haigh reporting the fact of the missing Mrs Durand-Deacon—was used, consciously or unconsciously, by him to exorcise a guilt with which he could no longer live—a remarkable example indeed of judicial euthanasia, suicide by hanging by courtesy of the Courts. To quote Lord Erskine, 'They mock the wisdom of the wisest in judicial trials'. Make no mistake, John George Haigh was a very complex creature—as were those many distinguished lawyers and doctors who failed to save Haigh's life. Lest the proposal sound inconceivable, it is worth recalling a passage in the excellent *Notable British Trials* series (published by W. Hodge), by Lord Dunboyne, in which he discusses the need to verify evidence—'a mere confession without other evidence would probably not suffice, but suppose a confession were made which contained a full description of the circumstances of the crime ... assistance of such a suicidal nature could scarcely be expected by the police from a prisoner before trial'. *Yet this was precisely the extent to which Haigh now chose to operate.*

It is a commonplace to reflect on the crude barbarism of past human activities, and attribute it all to simple ignorance, yet if the perceptive analysis of men such as Lord Erskine over 150 years ago, was accepted and believed even now, then the terrible act of final execution and death for human action, no matter how awful, must be unthinkable. There must be isolation from society for its protection, for society too has rights, but not the ultimate obscenity of taking life. Man cannot be blamed for seeking to simplify the nearly incomprehensible, the psycho-dynamics of human actions and decisions. The truth is that they cannot, even in our present state of knowledge, be so simplified into the clear-cut black and whiteness implicit in the McNaughton rules.

In many ways Haigh's whole life, taken in its intricate interwoven structure of the gentle, ruthless, unreliable, cruel, sentimental avaricious and generous, mirrors the personality and life-style of most men. It is unflattering and challenging to realise that, or to accept it, but it is still true. It is because of the many strands in the make-up of our personalities that the simple answer so beloved of the Courts and the judiciary, given under no matter what duress or rules of procedure, is frequently misleading. No one could say with any authority how Haigh arrived at his decision to shoot or kill his victims.

Haigh wrote that his youth had 'none of the joys or the companionship which small children usually have'. 'From my earliest years my recollection is of my father saying "Do not" or "There shall not". Any form of sport or light entertainment was frowned upon, and regarded as not edifying.' There was 'only and always, a condemnation and prohibition'. In essence this is a summary of his early childhood and youth. It is a record of benevolent repression and isolation; it is a record of an abnormal environment in which to rear a child. If we accept that environmental pressures acting on a genetically predisposed individual mould the life-style of the personality, then we can presume that Haigh's emotional development was distorted by this over-strict and rigid home life. This indeed was the perfect milieu for a repressed, disturbed mind which showed itself time and again from his earliest childhood, through his manhood, and finally in the strangely banal, dream-like, superficial content of his letters from the condemned cell to his parents and others. It is strange that if the defence was to be based on the fact that this man murdered because of a process of reasoning derived from an inbuilt dysfunction of reasoning, that the whole process of the distorted psychosexual development from his childhood on to manhood was not examined in greater detail. Why was it that the Attorney General and the trial judge, Mr Justice Humphreys, were permitted to dismiss the evidence submitted about Haigh's childhood as 'the word of a man who was utterly and completely unreliable'. His recitation of the murder process was in fact later proven to be correct in nearly every detail. So he did not lie all the time. Even had Haigh never told the truth, there were many persons, teachers, neighbours and others, who knew of the strange Plymouth Brethren upbringing and authoritarian family attitudes of the Haigh household. Why was no one called in evidence to support Haigh's own statements about the disturbing nature of his childhood? There was the understandably traumatic transition from the anti-clericalist, anti-institutional Puritanical religion of the Brethren to the period when he acted as the choirboy at Wakefield Cathedral's High Anglican services, laden with a heady ritual—everything that he had been taught to reject. Because of the educational advantages of a chorister, he was forced at a very early age to live the two widely disparate lives of Plymouth Brethren and High Church Anglicanism, an unendurably stressful experience for the child, for which he later suffered. He refers to a strange insistence by his father that the use of *Treasure Island* as a curricular subject at school was 'unfit for children, with pirates and murder', and his father's awesome devotion to the 'blood and horror of the Old Testament'. He was, he says, nurtured on Bible stories, 'mostly concerned with sacrifice'. There is no doubt whatever about these facts, and while it seems perfectly permissible for the prosecuting counsel to dismiss Haigh's reference to them, it is strange that more was not heard of the importance of this formative phase in Haigh's life, when an attempt was being made to establish the necessarily 'schizoid' (to use an old-fashioned term with a widely accepted lay meaning) nature of Haigh's later personality.

Again the enigma of man's true character as opposed to his public pose is well shown. A perfectly understandable comment in Lord Dunboyne's book is that 'Haigh did not appear to have developed any morbid sex traits in early adolescence, he still showed no signs of abnormality'. Yet he was, in fact, a solitary schoolboy. He became, it appears, an inveterate liar, because he came to realise that the truth often distressed his parents. He was lazy. He was an indifferent scholar, not an athlete, and had apparently been known to expose himself sexually on a number of occasions. My point is simply to show how difficult it is for us to look at one another and at a superficial level say this is normal, and that not. Haigh, even in childhood and early adolescence, was beginning to react to the stresses of the solitary life of a compulsive solitary fantasist. A matter of interest which will be dealt with later is the fact that he was married for a very brief time, only; He may have been introduced to sex life early and sewn his wild oats, but he then tired of sex'. Mr Justice Humphreys, in his summing-up, expressed relief that there was 'no sex element in the case'. That in fact was one of the strangest features of this whole case, and that it was accepted by the psychiatrist is another puzzling feature of the defence of Haigh, although it is only fair to say that if Dr Yellowlees had attempted to question the wisdom or accuracy of legal authorities referred to by the lawyers or the trial judge, or to dismiss them with the contempt with which the trial judge and lawyers dismissed the psychiatric evidence which did not suit the case for the prosecution, he would quickly have been reminded of his need to respect these authorities. The Attorney General dismissed psychiatric evidence—'we do not try them on speculation and theories unsupported by any kind of sworn testimony'—but what if complexity of human reasoning does not permit of the child-like belief that everything in life is either black or white and has a clear answer, and above all if certain proof is not possible one way or the other? This being so, in a case where a man's life is in the balance, surely he should be given the balance of doubt in his favour. Alternately, there is the trial judge's ingenious and facile dictum, 'It is the wicked mind of the man the criminal law says must be taken into consideration, *and for which he must be punished*' (my italics). Yet the Attorney General elicited the categorical statement from Dr Yellowlees, and it appears to have been accepted by the judge, that J.G.H. was a lunatic. 'You would call him a lunatic in ordinary everyday language?' Dr Yellowlees: 'Among doctors I would'. Does the legal process, from the police to the executioner, take any credit from killing an admitted lunatic? What was the purpose of the retention of Broadmoor, with its acceptance, contrary to the McNaughton rules, that a man can kill and because he is a lunatic not suffer execution, even before the whole terrible process of hanging was abolished by an enlightened society? It is not a fair assumption that Haigh was condemned to death as soon as he confessed at Chelsea Police Station to the six murders accepted as proven, and the three possible murders? The melodramatic hysteria of the newspaper 'human vampire' campaign, linked to Haigh's pathetic insistence on establishing for once in his life that he was not the immature, insecure personality end-product of a life and environment that ensured he would develop the psychopathic aberrations which patterned his grossly disturbed life-style from boyhood to his death on the gallows.

Why is it that Dr Yellowlees did not refuse to argue to simplify for the Court the diagnostic process in establishing that a person is mentally disturbed or insane? The Attorney General asked 'What objective sign of insanity is there apart from what the prisoner has said to you?' If there were none, that did not make him sane, and what about the barbarous murders as objective proof? Indeed, Dr Yellowlees helped to validate the Attorney

General's point when he asserted his conviction after his first interview of a mere twenty-five minutes, that J.G.H. suffered from 'a perfect example of pure paranoia', and went into Court to establish his insanity after three short interviews amounting to a total of about two hours, he made it all appear too simple and cursory. It is little wonder that Sir David Maxwell Fyfe's gallant attempt to establish Haigh's insanity was so easily demolished by the Attorney General.

Dr Yellowlees, it appears, became obsessed with the aptness of Professor Tanzi's description of the paranoid constitution and pure paranoia and its apparent suitability as a description of Haigh's mental condition. A detailed examination of Haigh, as a boy, adolescent, and man, and his grossly disturbed life-style, which in itself was the most eloquent vindication of his insanity, could not possibly have been elicited in three interviews lasting a mere two hours, and without extensive interviews in depth with everyone associated with him in his home, schools, business and elsewhere.

The trial Judge's behaviour was also of interest. It was said that the 'trial was tempered by that spirit of fairness to the accused with which the administration of the criminal law in modern England has become imbued.' May be so—yet it is pertinent to examine more closely the behaviour of those concerned in that process. Firstly, it has to be recalled that the Defence did not question the evidence for the prosecution as to the charge of murder against Haigh. It was accepted as proven. Therefore only one line of defence stood between Haigh and the hangman, and that was Dr Yellowlees and his evidence of insanity. In that case it seems to me that this witness, with his desperately serious responsibility, deserved especial grace, sympathy and patience.

There were a few incidents which could be further considered. For instance, the trial judge commented on Haigh's father's statement, 'John was a good boy . . . he got on well with other boys . . . there was nothing wrong mentally'. Clearly the father was a known ascetic and Puritanically rigidly religious man, whom we know had a fear relationship with his son, and we know too that the son had learned to lie to him. The result then surely was that this evidence was that of an honest, honourable man, but completely unreliable. That being so, the trial judge, instead of attempting to question his credibility, went on to reinforce it by his own comment, 'It is contrary to my experience that his (an accused's) relations in a murder, setting up a defence, are unwilling to help him by saying that there is a great deal of insanity in the family.' Clearly he was telling the jury to believe the father that Haigh was not insane. Indeed the poor father's evidence of sanity appears to have won an easier acceptance from the Court than that of the unfortunate expert witness, Dr Yellowlees. In this case, the process of break-down is quite remarkable. In his statement for the defence Dr Yellowlees appeared to be satisfied about Haigh's insanity. It is probable that his references to Haigh's 'callous, cheerful, bland, almost friendly indifference of the accused to crimes which he freely admits having committed is unique in my experience' helped to alienate any last possible scintilla of sympathy the Court or the public might have had for Haigh. Yet of course this feature of callous, cheerful indifference is one of the cardinal features of the psychopathic insanity of which Haigh's whole life-style was typical. It was tossed to the Court as a supplementary proof of what Lord Dunboyne in his *Notable Trials* book describes as 'the monstrous Haigh'. This feature, as with pain in a cancer, or paralysis in polio, if far from being 'unique' as described by Dr Yellowlees; it is a commonplace in the personality make-up of the psychopath. It was an integral manifestation of Haigh's insanity; it explained his total indifference to pain and suffering and gives some idea of the absurdity of attempting to apply the simple test of 'Did he know he did wrong, or didn't he?' That question could only be answered with any certainty if Haigh was sane, which all were agreed he was not. This is the point which the Court in my opinion should have established and shown to be the case; it surely owed this at least to Haigh.

If we examine Yellowlee's evidence there appears to be a failure to resist the Court's pressure to discount important features in the whole underlying psycho-pathology of these murders and Haigh's personality.

The general naïve Victorian prudery of Defence, Prosecution and trial judge at the hint that sex could enter into the murders is of interest. The Judge noted how relieved he was that there was to be no sex element to be advanced by the Defence. Sir David Maxwell Fyfe asked, 'Is there a complete absence of any sex element or interest in the accused?' Yellowlees: 'Yes, and that in itself is of course an abnormal thing.' Sir David Maxwell Fyfe: 'What significance do you attribute to the absence of sex?' Yellowlees: 'It is an indication of a very great abnormality of some kind.' Now these are very strong words, and developed could surely be an integral and important part of a defence of insanity. The uncontrollable nature of the sex drives in certain cases could not be unknown to the Courts. Yet Dr Yellowlees was unable to develop this theme. Sir David Maxwell Fyfe asked, 'This is not the kind of case where you are dependent on the sort of Viennese psychology that everything is related to sex?' Yellowlees: 'No, it has nothing to do with that'. Recall that this was happening in post-war London at a time when there was still a certain left-over prejudice that anything good could possibly emanate from an Axis country, and when there was a stranger resistance than exists today to an interpretation of human activity that takes account of unconscious sex drives. Yet surely it is the duty of the Court, especially in the circumstances where Lord Dunboyne tells us that the trial judge was thought privately to have believed that Haigh was sane, to exercise a particular concern on all issues. The shocking truth is that the Court, guided by its professional advisers in dismissing Viennese psychology, was treating with contempt at least two of the greatest authorities on the human mind and its actions—in Sigmund Freud, and Richard von Krafft-Ebing. Whatever the relevance of psychiatry to this case, surely the dismissal of the remarkably comprehensive collection of aberrant human behaviour whose origins were sexual in nature, in the famous collection of cases recorded under the title *Psychopathica Sexualis*, is unwise. There is indeed a record there of a case of a man whose aberrant sex activity included burning women's clothing with sulphuric acid. While it is not possible to give in detail the psycho-sexual dynamics of Haigh's life and death, anyone who knows of the staggeringly varied acts between men and women, and by men on women, in pursuit of sex satisfaction cannot possibly dismiss Haigh's life-style from his sexual self-exposure. His bizarre, brief marriage and his strange silence on the subject of sex, must bring anybody to share Dr Yellowlees' conclusion that the total pattern of his apparently absent normal sex life 'was an indication of a very great abnormality'—so great indeed that it is difficult to know why it was that he did not attempt to establish that Haigh was the victim of some macabre uncontrollable sado-masochistic sex drive which ensured that, although he knew that what he did was wrong, he could not control it. It seems to be totally absurd that the inexplicably complicated intricacies of the psycho-pathology of these murders should have been forced into the infantile strait-jacket of the McNaughton rules—if he knew he did wrong, and did it, then he must hang, as he did.

In Dr Yellowlees's place, I would not personally have concerned myself unduly with the 'horror film madman', a histrionic image which clearly the unfortunate Haigh introduced in order to establish the yellow-press melodramatisation of him as a divinely directed, blood-sucking, callous human vampire. These relatively unimportant features of the case, whether true or not, seem to have fascinated and understandably repelled the Court and the public. From the psychiatric viewpoint they were of relative importance only. While these aspects of the case provoked the anger of the ignorant, were they true they should in fact have only added to the compassion and pity that this unfortunate man deserved. These tragic murders were committed by a man who was the end-product of two influences—genetic pre-disposition, and his environment and upbringing, for neither of which he could be held responsible, and yet we hanged him.

One answer to the 'cold-blooded psychopath' incidentally is this: that such a person is in fact an individual of remarkable gentleness and sensitivity—Haigh's letters from jail give evidence of this—who has been hurt often by society. He is a man whose psyche is so excoriated, raw, and painful, that he is unable to establish a lasting relationship with anyone. This Haigh never seems to have been able to do.

At the same time, it was not an *angry* judge or jury who condemned this man to death. It was a Court which on the medical evidence, acting within the McNaughton rules, did so. An examination of this evidence is of interest. Sir David Maxwell Fyfe made an eloquent and well-argued case for the defence. In the opinion of Lord Dunboyne it appeared to be based on the case made by Lord Erskine in the defence of Hadfield, who shot at King George III. It was the general belief that Hadfield was insane, and wished to be put to death. What went wrong?

There were three medical experts appointed under section 2(4) of the Criminal Justice Act of 1884, to enquire into Haigh's sanity. They concluded that there was not the slightest reason to believe Haigh was irresponsible according to legal standards, or insane according to medical standards. What could the Court or the Home Secretary do except execute Haigh on 10th August, 1949? Yet we know the old saying, that 'doctors differ, and patients die.' We know nothing of the depth or extent of the examinations carried out by them in order to reach this verdict in such an obscure and strange series of murders—at least Dr Yellowlees gave Haigh two hours of his time. How do we reconcile this decision of clear sanity, with Dr Yellowlee's evidence? Early in the case Sir David Maxwell Fyfe established a number of points as to Haigh's mental condition. There is a phrase of Burke's which talks of 'admiring the plumage but ignoring the dying bird', which springs to mind as one marvels at the economy, directness and lethal efficiency with which the Attorney General conducted his questioning of Dr Yellowlees.

Let us refer back to the case as presented by Sir David Maxwell Fyfe and note the strand-by-strand weave of the rope of cross-examination, which ended in Haigh's conviction and execution. The Defence Counsel gave his thoughtful analysis of the findings which led to the broad defence that Haigh was a man of paranoid constitution who had become a case of pure paranoia and murdered because he was insane; compelling indeed as was this argument, it could not save Haigh's life unless Dr Yellowlees was allowed to question the relevance to contemporary psychiatric thinking of the nineteenth-century McNaughton rules. If these rules were applied rigidly then the verdict must be Guilty. Why did the Defence not try to establish that there are many precedents within the Commonwealth countries where British laws applied where the McNaughton rules were no longer accepted on a capital charge? Dr Yellowlees made the case that 'Haigh was of paranoid constitution and was suffering from some of the symptoms of pure paranoia', which, he continued was 'a profound mental disease'. The trial judge conceded this point. 'Let us assume that it is a disease', the jury were told; but the McNaughton rules demanded simply that when he committed a crime a man must be 'labouring under a defect of reason and that such a defect of reason arose from a disease of the mind.' According to Dr Yellowlees after his first interview with Haigh, he had no doubt at all about his paranoid constitution. 'Haigh', he said, 'had no special interest in right or wrong or in the laws of the country', an admission of special interest in later cross-examination. Haigh also said that he did not believe that murder in his case was punishable by law. In reply to a question as to whether Haigh genuinely believed whatever he said to be true, Yellowlees answered, 'The one thing he is not is a malingerer'. 'Does he appear to believe it?' 'Yes, absolutely.' 'He thinks he ought not to be punished?' 'Yes.'

Having established these clear and unequivocal statements about Haigh, Yellowlees then faced the Attorney General, whose opening and most damaging broadside disclosed that the witness did not know whether he had seen Haigh three or five times in jail. This had a clearly demoralising effect on Yellowlees, and certainly cannot have helped him with the jury. The Attorney General then appeared to show the discrepancy between Professor Tanzi's and Dr Yellowlees' criteria for paranoia. His most damaging cross-examination however was restricted to the Court's main concern, an insistence that the McNaughton rules be applied in the case. The Attorney General pressed him on the knowledge of the quality of the act, the murder, 'Did you believe that what he was doing was wrong?' 'I think it is very doubtful . . . I think he was acting under a guidance of a higher power, but I do not know.' Repeatedly, to further queries, Dr Yellowlees quite honestly replied, 'I do not know'. How indeed could anyone know with certainty how Haigh's tortured mind reasoned its way through his terrible acts? When again asked, however, whether Haigh knew that murder was punishable and wrong by the law of the country, Dr Yellowlees replied, 'Yes, I think he knew that'.

Here the Defence case collapsed, since under the McNaughton rules the jury needed hardly to take the fifteen minutes they did to find Haigh guilty. Under pressure, Yellowlees had abandoned his original assured position about this insane lunatic and grossly abnormal personality. Badgered by the judge, deflated by Shawcross, it is not surprising that he was, metaphorically, almost forced to don the Black Cap himself.

A simple illustration of the weakness of the McNaughton rules can be seen in the case of a suicide, which after all is self-murder and was once wrong in law. Yet we all know that given certain transient emotionally stressful situations, the urge to suicide can be uncontrollable. The man who survives a suicide attempt is not now punished and may be considered completely sane, yet have attempted self-murder—we no longer punish the successful suicide with a stake through his chest. In a criminal case* I would cite the dilemma of an obsessional vegetarian, convinced of the wrongness of the slaughtering of animals for human consumption. He burns down an abattoir, costing tens of thousands of pounds. He knows the act is wrong in the eyes of the law of the land, and punishable by imprisonment, but the act of arson is not wrong for him. This case is childishly simple compared to the tragic intricacies of the devious psycho-pathology of Haigh's grossly distorted personality which led him to murder

* This is not an hypothetical case, but one in which Dr Browne was called as witness for the defence. A.L.B.

men and women, and violate as he did the bodies of his victims. Did it really need a battery of psychiatrists or a court of law to decide that the unfortunate man was quite mad? or as Dr Yellowlees said at one stage of his evidence, 'Yes, a lunatic.' Yet they hanged that lunatic.

Haigh, his Parents and the Bible

And so on the *tenth** day of August, 1949, John George Haigh went to his death. He was no Mordecai and so there was no Esther to intercede with the king on his behalf, causing a Haman (or a Home Secretary) to die on the gallows he had himself erected.

The only persons who could intercede were the members of the Medical Panel of Statutory Inquiry, consisting of Dr W. Norwood East, formerly Medical Commissioner of the Prison Commission, Dr J. F. Hopwood, Medical Superintendent of Broadmoor, and Dr Murdoch of Wandsworth Prison, the latter having been called back from his holidays in Scotland to attend. This Panel advised the Home Secretary that Haigh was sane in law and that consequently there was no reason why sentence of death should not be carried out according to that law.

Leslie Ingham Shyder, the prison surgeon, was to examine the body and pronounce life extinct, and to sign the grim certificate which a prison officer posted outside at ten minutes past nine, hundreds of people surging forward to read it.

* I italicise the date, because *The Concise Encyclopedia of Crime and Criminals* (André Deutsch 1961) repeats the same error as the Notable British Trials series, giving the date as August 6th. This Encyclopaedia was edited by Sir Harold Scott, former Scotland Yard chief!

Those who were really interested could have obtained an additional thrill by taking a bus from Wandsworth to Madame Tussaud's where the effigy of Haigh was making its début in the Chamber of Horrors in the same suit he had worn at his trial, details correct down to his mother's hand-knitted, double-heeled socks about which he had raised 'merry hell' when the laundry at Brixton lost three pairs. Despite the meticulous attention to detail, the model of Haigh does not bear the startling resemblance to the original which is a feature of most effigies in that famous hall of the infamous. It depicts Haigh with the suggestion of a sneer on his face, whereas in life he was rarely seen without a smile. Haigh himself had asked Stafford Somerfield to give the suit to Madame Tussaud's.

At the inquest the cause of death was given as 'by judicial hanging' and Haigh's weight as 10 stone 10 pounds. Dr F. E. Camps, pathologist, said Haigh was a perfectly healthy man.

Mr R. B. Harvey Watt, the Coroner, said: 'I have heard it said that inquiries are unnecessary because everybody knows the cause of death. But it is really a half-truth. We are here to represent and see that the sentence which was passed has been properly carried out.'*

According to the law of the land existing at that time, there had been no terrible miscarriage of justice in the sentence of death carried out on Haigh, not a judicial crime of the magnitude that hanged Evans and, on another occasion, Bentley; both mentally retarded; both innocent. Haigh was guilty. He knew it. The whole country knew it before he even stood trial and an editor was sent to gaol for telling the country just that, so it is difficult to understand how any jury, Sussex or otherwise, could have had an open mind on the subject.

Haigh was the only son of two religious maniacs who never sinned and who saw a miracle in his birth, tried to bring him up to be, even as Mordecai, a 'perfect and upright man, one that feareth

* At one time, of course, a representative of the Press Association had to be present at hangings to make doubly sure that the sentence was 'properly carried out'.

God and escheweth evil'. They themselves believed implicitly every word they read in their Bible. This son, who was born when the mother was forty, was taught to believe likewise. In the Book of Kings he read that a good woman, in a time of famine, confessed: 'So we boiled my son and did eat him.' He read of soldiers who ripped up the bellies of women who were with child. He read of sacrifices and seventy human heads in seventy baskets. He read that two eunuchs threw Jezebel out of a window and that the dogs ate her 'and there were none to bury her'.

There is not the remotest connection between Jezebel and the highly respectable Mrs Durand-Deacon, who was Haigh's last victim, but was there not a possible tenuous connection in Haigh's mind with the incident of the eunuchs throwing Jezebel out of the window, leaving her unburied, and his own pouring the sludge of Mrs Durand-Deacon's dissolved remains onto the ground outside his 'workshop' at Crawley?

Haigh confessed to nine murders, but to my mind his own mother made a confession of more profound importance than the story he told detectives at Chelsea Police Station on the night of February 28th, 1949. On her death-bed, she said to the man to whom she gave her son's death-cell letters for safe keeping, 'We despised the villagers because we thought we were the elect of God. But we were not.'

This is both the crux and the clue. They thought they were the elect of God and despised their neighbours because of it. Was not this in itself a form of madness—a form of madness which manifested itself in their son at an early age, but in a different way? They showed their contempt for their neighbours by 'keeping themselves to themselves', arrogating to themselves the right to banish other 'Saints' from the chapel. As a boy, Haigh spat down on the heads of people ascending or descending the tramcar on which he was travelling to school.

The Nazis began by spitting at a few Jews. They ended by exterminating six million of them.

Mr and Mrs Haigh were religious to the point of mania but

they did not teach their son to Love Thy Neighbour. From them he learned to despise his neighbour.

Although Haigh had a number of girl friends in his later years, the relationships were platonic, not sexual. It is more than possible, in fact it is probable that Mrs Haigh firmly instructed her 'Sonnie'to regard every girl as a Jezebel. Perhaps this would explain his habit of indecently exposing himself to schoolgirls on the tramcar. Even when he is in his late thirties, having served three prison sentences, we have the evidence of Mrs Haigh admonishing him: 'What right has Mrs Henderson to buy you socks?'

It is still the custom in many parts of England to lower the household blinds when a death occurs. It needs no great stretch of the imagination to see the blinds lowered at the house in Stainburn Drive, Leeds, on the morning of August 10th, 1949, shutting out every ray of sunlight. It needs even less imagination to see two frail, octogenarians on their knees, hands clasped in prayer, grey heads bowed as the city clocks struck nine.

They were no longer proud, but sorely afflicted. Their disillusionment was complete and utter. Now they were humbled and completely crushed. They who had despised their neighbours were too ashamed to venture into the street, too ashamed to go out to buy a card for their son's last birthday, delegating this delicate, poignant and well-nigh impossible task to the brother of the man who, thirty years previously, had to wait on the doorstep of their little house in Ledger Lane, Outwood, before accompanying Sonnie to school.

Justice had been done and had been seen to be done. Society was avenged, but the full and dreadful majesty of the Law had not succeeded in punishing John George Haigh. He smiled at the end. The Law had punished his parents.

The Law said Haigh was sane. Of course he was sane. He was as sane as a Kray. He was as sane as Mitchell the Axe. He was as sane as Straffen. He was as sane as any man who bequeaths his best suit to Madame Tussaud's. Surely this last act—and act is the right word—bears out Dr Noël Browne's suggestion that he might even have looked forward to the drama of his own execution? Remember, too, that he had asked for a rehearsal.

Apart from those officially connected with the final macabre scene, the last man from the outside world to talk to Haigh was Stafford Somerfield, who asked him, 'Tell me, what's the real story? It's no use pretending now.'

'You've got the real story,' Haigh replied. 'I was impelled to kill by wild blood dreams. The spirit inside me commanded me to kill.'

It was Somerfield's impression that no normal man could have behaved as Haigh did during his last hours on earth, which brings us back to the vexatious question, Who is normal? More important, who is sane and who is insane?

'The Law does not purport or presume to define insanity,' the late Lord Chief Justice Hewart once pontificated. 'That is a medical question. What the Law considers is the conditions which have to be satisfied in order that a person may be excused from criminal responsibility; that is a legal question.'

One hundred and six years before Haigh was hanged, the American psychiatrist, Isaac Ray, declared that no matter how one chose to define insanity it was not something that should depend upon the academics of English judges.

Exactly one hundred and ten years after Ray's pronouncement, and four years after the execution of Haigh, the Royal Commission on Capital Punishment reported: 'The test of criminal responsibility contained in the McNaughton Rules cannot be defended in the light of modern medical knowledge and modern penal views.'

There are those of not inconsiderable numbers who tenaciously hold the view that, sane or insane, the Haighs of the world should be put down rather than put away—'and good riddance'. It is perhaps platitudinous to reply that, if human life is to be regarded as sacred, then it should be regarded as such on all levels. Otherwise we might as well revert to the barbarism of the Bible—the good book in which Haigh had been taught to believe implicitly.

Plymouth Brethren, the religious sect to which Haigh's parents belonged, were known as the Peculiar People. It began in Devon, hence its name, and spread to various parts of the country, like a spiritual smallpox; and, like smallpox, it left scars.

The late Sir Edmund Gosse, a far more distinguished, literate and articulate person than Haigh, was also the only child of Plymouth Brethren parents. His father, Philip Henry Gosse, the zoologist, did not marry until he was 38; his bride, Emily Bowes, was four years older. Yet she conceived a son and Gosse's father recorded the event in his diary, thus: 'E. delivered of son. Received green swallow from America.'

In his minor classic, *Father and Son, A Study of Two Temperaments*, Edmund Gosse recalls a childhood memory of a meeting of the Plymouth Brethren:

'I was awakened in the pitchy night to go off with my father to the Room, where a scanty gathering held a penitential prayer meeting. We came home as dawn was breaking, and in the process of time sat down to breakfast, which consisted—at that dismal hour—of slices of dry bread and a tumbler of cold water each. During the morning I was not allowed to paint, or write, or withdraw to my study in the box room. . . . Our midday meal came at last, the meal was strictly confined, as before, the dry slices of the loaf and a tumbler of water.'

It should not be inferred from the above that either Gosse or Haigh was brought up strictly on a diet of bread and water. Between penitential prayer meetings, there is no doubt that they were both adequately nourished. Yet Gosse's story does seem to bear out Haigh's recollection of being put on a bread and water diet by his fanatically religious parents, a diet far more Spartan than he ever endured in prison. For a man who was alleged in court to be 'incapable of telling the truth', Haigh succeeded in telling it on quite a number of occasions. As Dr Browne points out, Haigh's confession was sufficiently truthful in its essentials to get him hanged.

More important than Gosse's account of the prayer meeting and the subsequent bread and water diet is a revealing and perspicacious remark about himself as a boy: 'I suppose that my queer reputation for sanctity, half-dreadful, half-ridiculous, surrounded me with a non-conforming atmosphere.'

This observation could be applied with equal force, perhaps even more so, to the young Haigh. In Haigh's case, the half-dreadful became the dreadful. In disposing of his victims, he was as pitiless as his father had been when casting out brother 'Saints' as if they were serpents.

One question has not been answered regarding Haigh's trial. He was taken into custody on February 28th, 1949. Yet on April 27th, almost exactly two calendar months later, Sir David Maxwell Fyfe made application to have the trial postponed because 'some scientific evidence was awaited'.

The evidence awaited was that of Dr Henry Yellowlees, the only witness called for the defence. Yet the first time that Dr Yellowlees saw Haigh was on July 1st, more than four months after Haigh was arrested and more than two months after Sir David asked to have the trial postponed. How could Sir David say that the defence was awaiting 'scientific evidence' on April 27th when on that date Dr Yellowlees had not even set eyes on Haigh, let alone interviewed him? What was the defence doing in the four months before Dr Yellowlees went to see Haigh?

I find this the most disturbing aspect of the case. It is a question that will probably never be answered because Sir David Maxwell Fyfe is dead and Dr Yellowlees refuses to comment.

Haigh had chosen Sir David Maxwell Fyfe as his counsel because he was attracted by the biblical connotation of his first name. But the legal David's ammunition was not as effective as that of his biblical namesake.

During the War, when a fire-watcher, Haigh had been blown from one roof on to another by the blast of a landmine. He escaped injury by miraculously falling onto sandbags. On August 10th, 1949, there was nothing to soften the impact of his drop.

Index